NEW YORK HARBOR

ANDREW BRITTON

The
History
Press

First published 2014

The History Press · The Mill · Brimscombe Port · Stroud · Gloucestershire · GL5 2QG
www.thehistorypress.co.uk

British Library Cataloguing in Publication Data.
A catalogue record for this book is available from the British Library.

ISBN 978 0 7524 9870 6

Typesetting and origination by The History Press
Printed in India

Cover illustrations: Front: SS *America* against the dramatic backdrop of Manhattan.
Back: New York Central Railroad steam tugboat No. 18. Both Britton Collection.

Left: This is an aerial view of New York Harbor on 11 September 1948, taken
from 8 miles high by an experimental XR-12 plane. The area seen is approximately
130 square miles. *United States Air Force/Associated Press*

Above: New York & New Jersey port map. *Matthew J. Britton*

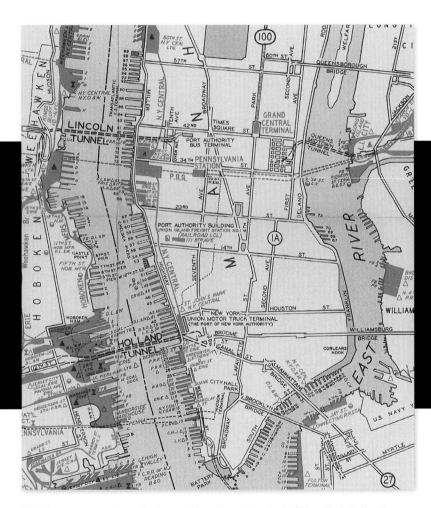

This closer-up map shows the Luxury Liner Row piers. *Port of New York Authority*

CONTENTS

	Introduction	4
	Acknowledgements	6
1	A History of New York Harbor	7
2	Around the Port	49
3	Tribute to the Tugboats	107
4	Railroad Ferries	117

TO BE LANDED AT **NEW YORK**
1st CUNARD LINE
SALOON BAGGAGE FOR
NAME
PER SS
DATE OF SAILING
FROM (PORT)
FINAL DESTINATION
DECK
STATE ROOM Nº
WANTED ON THE VOYAGE
TO BE LANDED AT **NEW YORK**

INTRODUCTION

NEW YORK HARBOR has long had a special place in the history of the Britton family. My grandfather, Alfred Britton, was the Leader of the Band on the Cunard White Star liners in the early twentieth century. In 1912 my grandfather was due to sail to New York on the maiden voyage of the RMS *Titanic*, but after he and my grandmother had watched the new liner enter Ocean Dock at Southampton on completion of her sea trials, there was a last-minute change of mind. They watched *Titanic* meander her way into dock and as the liner entered Ocean Dock she sucked in the water and created a vacuum, causing a ship that was tied up to knock into her. That night, ahead of the doomed maiden voyage, my grandmother had a chilling premonition, woke up and begged my grandfather not to get on board *Titanic,* which was sailing next day to New York. Had he taken the job, these words may not have been written and he would have no doubt gone down with his musicians playing 'Nearer my God to thee'.

My grandfather was to sail from Southampton to New York many times in subsequent years as Leading Violinist and Leader of the Band on many transatlantic liners and he was joined by his son, my uncle Norman Britton, as a pianist. During the late 1950s and early 1960s another family member, my uncle Joe Webb, worked on the Cunard RMS *Queen Elizabeth*, and he, along with family friend Sid Deeming who worked on the P&O liners, would return home with exciting stories about their visits to New York. The family would listen in awe and wonder to their tales of a cavalcade of liners docked along the piers of the Atlantic piers in New York, known as Luxury Liner Row. We would marvel on learning how the liners battled their way up the Hudson through the ice, gallantly assisted by the Moran tugboats. We listened attentively to accounts of the inter-ship football matches played at New York where there was a competition for the Transatlantic Cup. I felt New York was in my blood and was somewhere I should learn more about.

Uncle Joe would often relate that the people of New York were very generous. He recalled the contrast in conditions of post-war life between Britain and the USA when he went ashore off the RMS *Queen Elizabeth* at Pier 90. Back in Southampton his family were surviving on strict rations, whereas in New York he would frequent the Market Diner in 11th Avenue for a slap-up steak meal, which he said would last him a week! Uncle Joe would frequently stock up with nylon stockings, which were well sought-after in Britain, to take back home to my Auntie Jean. His brother Bernard Webb, who worked on both the RMS *Mauretania* and RMS *Queen Mary*, recalled that New Yorkers would generously invite visiting

Cunard sailors into their homes and treat them like royalty. He too would fill his case with plentiful US supplies to distribute to the family.

As I flew over New York Harbor in a jet aircraft, when accompanying my eldest son Jonathan to a soccer tournament in Atlanta, I peered down at the great city to point out the Hudson River, the harbour and piers. Immediately a lump came into my throat and I was filled with emotion as I remembered my family and favourite liners: the SS *United States*, RMS *Queen Mary*, RMS *Queen Elizabeth*, RMS *Mauretania*, SS *France*, SS *Liberté* and SS *Ile de France*. Oh, how I wished I could turn the clock back and I dreamt of recording those days for others to enjoy in a book. Now, some years on, that dream has come true. Here is the book, which I dedicate to my eldest son, Jonathan.

Love life, love New York and the memory of the ocean liners.

A portrait of the author's grandfather, Alfred J. Britton, with his violin. He was Leader of the Band on many White Star Line Atlantic ocean liners operating from Southampton to New York. *Ruth Pringle Collection*

ACKNOWLEDGEMENTS

I guess this book would not have been written had it not been for my family, particularly my late father, who encouraged my interest in ocean liners. My sister, Ruth Pringle, has been of considerable assistance, allowing me access to the family archives to trace my grandfather's and uncles' voyages to New York and supplying old black-and-white photographs. Ruth has also encouraged me throughout when researching, with great suggestions. Perhaps it is my Uncle Joe, late of the Cunard RMS *Queen Elizabeth*, with his wonderful stories of visits to New York, to whom I owe the greatest debt of thanks. His accounts of New York Harbor in the great days of ocean liners in the 1950s and '60s inspired me enormously.

Considerable assistance with illustrations and information has been received from David Boone, Ernest Arroyo, Jim Gavin, Richard Faber, the Braun Brothers Estate and the Associated Press of the United States. Over a number of years I have made myself a thorough nuisance to these individuals and newspaper editors at the *New York Times*, *Washington Post*, *USA Today*, *Chicago Tribune* and Historic Images Archives, but I kept my promise to you all. Thank you.

A special thank you must go to Jim McFaul and Roy Cressey of the World Ship Society for their considerable assistance. Hisashi Noma of the World Ship Society of Japan also contributed superb colour views of ships entering New York and I am extremely grateful to him.

My brother-in-law, Mike Pringle, has meticulously scanned and restored the slides and illustrations in this book. Additionally, Mike has photographed original paintings, diagrams, sketches and artefacts. His generous help has been invaluable.

Michael Jakeman has once again readily offered his assistance and expertise in proofreading this book. His enormous, unbridled help and indispensable sharp eye for detail has proved essential.

I must say a big thank you to my wife Annette for supporting me on a daily basis when researching and writing this book and also my sons Jonathan, Mark and Matthew for all their help.

A HISTORY OF NEW YORK HARBOR

New York Harbor is on the east coast of the USA and consists of the waterways around the estuary of the Hudson River where it empties into New York Bay. It is one of the most important ports in the world and can trace its origins back to the sixteenth century, when Giovanni da Verrazzano anchored here in what is now called The Narrows in 1524 and was greeted by a canoe party of the native Lenape population who used New York Harbor for fishing.

In 1609 Henry Hudson entered New York Harbor from the Atlantic Ocean and began to explore north, along the river that now bears his name. His preliminary survey encouraged others to explore the local area and engage in trade with the Lenape people. However, it was not until 1624 that the first permanent European settlement was established on Governor's Island, followed by a settlement on Brooklyn eight years later. European colonists quickly discovered the geological attributes that made New York Harbor so hospitable as a potential centre of future commerce. The construction of the first wharf, named Schreyers Hook Dock, on the Manhattan bank of the lower East River, was completed in 1648 under the direction of Peter Stuyvesant, the colonial Dutch Director-General. This sheltered location established New York as a leading 'New World' port on the Eastern Seaboard of the continent.

The Eighteenth Century

When the American War of Independence broke out in April 1775, the British decided that 'decisive action' should be taken against New York using forces recruited throughout the British Empire, as well as mercenary troops hired from German states. The British took control of New York Harbor and New York City until the war ended in 1783. When the British declared an end to hostilities on 4 February 1783 it signalled it was time for British loyalists to depart from New York and so, on 26 April, 7,000 loyalists set sail from New York to Canada.

By 1800 most of the southern tip of Manhattan had been developed with landfill to allow the construction of piers and wharves along the shoreline. The city conurbation began to spread north as a result. The next major development in the history of the Port of New York was in 1824, when the first American dry dock was built on the East River. From this date the port began to expand rapidly, with the introduction of new steam-powered ships and the completion, in 1825, of the Erie Canal. By 1840, New York was established as the premier port of the USA, with more passengers and a greater tonnage of cargo entering the port than any other in the country. As a result the city boomed.

Viewed from the decks of the approaching Moran tugboat *Grace Moran*, the impressive stern of the American Export Lines SS *Independence*, emblazoned with the words '*Independence* New York', bobs up and down in the waves. The *Independence* is anchored just beyond the Narrows in New York Upper Bay awaiting the Sandy Hook pilot. *Britton Collection*

At the approach to the Narrows and the entrance to New York Harbor, the weather conditions could often change. Here we see the waves becoming choppy with some bow spray as the TS *Bremen* slows approaching the Ambrose Lightship. Note the wooden decks and the ship's bell. *Britton Collection*

Brooklyn's harbour facilities developed at a more leisurely pace. The shoreline from Brooklyn Bridge southwards to Bay Ridge was the first major development with a marshy area drained and excavated to allow the construction of the Atlantic Basin, the Erie Basin and Brooklyn Naval Yards. The development of port facilities along the New Jersey side of the harbour was considerably hampered by mudflats and tidal marshes. These challenges were met by extensive dredging, landfill and drainage. Today this once rich environmental habitat has evolved and transformed to become the most densely populated area in the United States.

American Civil War 1861–1865

During the American Civil War of 1861 to 1865, New York Harbor was said to be bustling with troops, supplies and equipment for the Union Army. New York was a fertile source for recruits to the Army as European immigrants stepped off the deck of ships and straight into action with a rifle. Alternatively, the newly arrived immigrant signed up to serve in the Brooklyn Navy Yard repairing Union ships. By the second year of hostilities the yard had expanded to employ over 6,000 men.

Amongst the military innovations during the Civil War period was the 'Wig-Wag Signalling' system, which used flags and, at night, kerosene lamps. It was tested in New York Harbor by Major Albert J. Myer. Measures were also taken around the harbour shores for protection against any possible Confederate attack with the construction and reinforcement of Army forts. Secret agents from the Confederacy based in New York provided information throughout the war on troop strengths and movements of shipping in the harbour. Some of these agents plotted to disrupt the Election Day in November 1864, but their plans were foiled by a double-agent. However, on 25 November the agents finally struck, setting fire to several hotels and other landmarks. The conspirators eventually fled north to Canada.

The Development of New York Harbor 1880–1914

In 1880 the engineer George Greene submitted development plans for the construction of four new piers on the Hudson River waterfront between West 19th and 22nd Streets. His visionary plans for the Chelsea area were designed to accommodate the new, longer transatlantic steamships from Europe. The plans were modified in 1889 and the construction

The most impressive skyline in the world forms the backdrop to the scene as the reactivated USS *West Virginia* sails from the Brooklyn Naval Yard on 22 April 1939. *Associated Press*

The White Star Line *Olympic*, on which Alfred J. Britton was Leader of the Band, is seen at Pier 59 in New York. *Education Department/Britton Collection*

Above: The United States Dreadnought battleship *Utah* is pictured entering the Brooklyn Navy dry dock on 19 May 1912. This was the first vessel to use the new $2.8 million dry dock, which at the time was the largest such facility in the USA. *Associated Press*

Left: The *Olympic* at Pier 59 in New York. This four-funnel liner was the sister of the *Titanic*. *New York Education Department/Britton Collection*

of the Chelsea Piers commenced in 1902, with completion in 1910. The finger-like, 800ft-long Chelsea Piers were impressive architectural structures with their elaborate ornamental roof façades. A member of the crew of the new British Cunard 790ft-long sister liners *Mauretania* and *Lusitania*, was so impressed that he likened them to the Victorian London railway terminal buildings. The New York public were also impressed with the new four-funnel British liners when they docked at the new Chelsea Piers. The following year, 1911, New Yorkers were enthralled and many cheered when the *Olympic*, with her new indoor swimming pool, arrived on her maiden voyage. The first liner to exceed 900ft, the *Aquitania* surpassed all with decorative touches of English Tudor, Baroque and Palladian splendour.

On 16 April 1912 crowds had been expected to gather in eager anticipation at the Chelsea Piers for the scheduled arrival from Southampton of the new White Star Line *Titanic*, on her maiden voyage. However, the joy on the faces of well-wishers, families and friends of those on board, anticipating the arrival of the superliner, soon changed to anxious worry as news began to filter through of the disaster as sea. As the minutes and hours ticked by the crowds swelled and eventually confirmation came through that the 'unsinkable' *Titanic* had sunk after striking an iceberg, with the loss of 1,500 lives. The *Carpathia* instead used the Chelsea Piers to land some of the survivors.

The First World War 1914–1918

Three years later, in May 1915, the *Lusitania* sailed from the 14th Street Pier in New York on her scheduled voyage to Liverpool. On the afternoon of 7 May, a German submarine was lurking 11 miles off the south-west coast of Ireland and torpedoed the former Blue Riband-winning liner. An internal explosion sent the stricken liner to the bottom in just under eighteen minutes, claiming the lives of 1,198 people. This action is said to have contributed to the United States later entering the First World War.

Isolation was a long tradition in the United States and when the First World War broke out, the feeling in New York was, why get involved in Europe's self-destruction? In the early days of the war, as Britain and France struggled against Germany, the intention in New York was to continue to trade with all sides as before. The British Royal Navy had other ideas and imposed a blockade on Germany. The results of this blockade were astonishing as US trade with Britain and France more than tripled between 1914 and 1916, while its trade with Germany was reduced by 90 per cent. It was this situation that prompted submarine warfare by the Germans.

In April 1917 the United States entered the war. The effect of this on New York Harbor was massive, as a seemingly infinite supply of fresh American soldiers and provisions were shipped across the Atlantic. The contribution of the US Navy to the war effort, with extra food and fuel sent from the Port of New York, is viewed by many historians as a decisive factor in the outcome of the First World War.

After the First World War, the war hero Sergeant Alvin York landed at Hoboken in New Jersey and was welcomed with a rapturous reception with an escort of tugs and pleasure craft. Ships around the port blew their whistles in salute and crowds lined the shores to wave. Sergeant York was one of the most decorated US soldiers of the First World War, having received the Medal of Honour for leading an attack on a German machine-gun nest, taking thirty-two machine guns, killing twenty-eight German soldiers and capturing 132 others. A group of Tennesseans living in New York arranged five-day-long celebrations. He stayed at the Waldorf Astoria and toured the New York subway system in a special car before continuing to Washington.

The Interwar Years 1919–1939

In 1919 proposals were put forward for a terminal facility at Stapleton, Staten Island and to develop the waterfront in Flushing Bay, Queens. Two years later, in 1921, the Port Authority of New York was created, initially as a planning agency. Historically there had been disputes between the states of New Jersey and New York over rail freight, shipping lanes and boundaries. The railway lines terminated on the New Jersey side of New York Harbor, whilst shipping was centred on Manhattan and Brooklyn. Consequently, freight had to be shipped across the Hudson River in barges. In 1916 the dispute over issues of rail freight resulted in New Jersey launching a lawsuit against New York. The outcome was that the Interstate Commerce Commission issued a directive to both states that they work together for the public interest and in 1917 the Harbor Development Commission recommended that a bi-state authority be established. The new Port Authority of New York and New Jersey has a geographical district of 1,500 square miles in New York Harbor with approximately a 25-mile radius of the Statue of Liberty. In 1925 the Port Authority was authorised to plan and construct bridges and take over the construction of the Holland Tunnel.

Uncle Norman Britton with his Cunard White Star Band pictured on board one of the Atlantic liners of the 1920s and '30s that operated from Southampton to New York. *Ruth Pringle Collection*

The evolution of the Port of New York and New Jersey along its 650-mile shoreline established eleven ports: Manhattan, Brooklyn, Queens, the Bronx, Staten Island, New Jersey, Bayonne, Newark, Jersey City, Hoboken and Weehawken. In its heyday the port boasted 1,800 docks, piers and wharves. Additionally, the Port of New York had thirty-nine civilian shipyards and the gigantic US Navy Shipyard on the East River. The port's thirty-nine large dry docks were the envy of the world and are said to have made certain the outcome of the Second World War in Europe.

Above: An evocative picture of America's first superliner, the SS *Leviathan*, is seen here sailing from New York on 5 January 1924, assisted by a flotilla of steam tugs. *Chicago Daily News/Associated Press*

Left: A superb aerial view of the maiden voyage arrival at New York of the Cunard White Star Line RMS *Queen Mary* in May 1936. *New York Education Department/Britton Collection*

Second World War 1939–1945

At the outbreak of the Second World War in Europe on 3 September 1939, the Cunard RMS *Queen Mary* was en route across the Atlantic to New York with her biggest ever peacetime compliment of passengers. Her sister, RMS *Queen Elizabeth*, was sitting in the fitting-out basin in Scotland and was a potential easy target for the German Luftwaffe bombers. As soon as the *Queen Mary* arrived in New York, her passengers disembarked and the majority of her crew were sent home to England. All reservations for return passage to Southampton were cancelled. The *Queen Mary* remained tied up at Pier 90 under secure guard and free of the threat of the German U-boats. She was quickly joined by the Cunard RMS *Mauretania*, which was similarly securely tied up in the neutral port.

The French Line *Normandie*, under the command of Captain Hervé Lehude, also arrived at Pier 88 in New York to seek a safe haven and tied up alongside the *Queen Mary* and *Mauretania*. The big question in New York was, would the new *Queen Elizabeth* sail across the Atlantic to join this distinguished gathering?

Back on the Clyde, Captain John Townley, the Master of the *Queen Elizabeth*, discovered that he was to sail the world's largest passenger liner unfinished, without sufficient lifeboats and fitted with the new Swedish-designed anti-magnetic de-gaussing anti-mine cable. Five hours after leaving the fitting-out basin, at 5.15 p.m. the new liner reached the Tail of the Bank at Greenock where she anchored off. The following day the ship was officially handed over to Cunard in the third-class dining saloon with a few drams of Scottish whisky. This was an unprecedented event as Cunard had been forced to accept a new ship without any tests or sea trials!

The crew (most of them recruited from the *Aquitania*) was mustered and they thought that they were to sail south, down the Irish Sea to Southampton for dry docking and the fitting out of the ship. They were in for a surprise, for Captain Townley informed them that they were to make an ocean voyage. No port of destination was mentioned in his address to the crew, but the Master of the *Elizabeth* had a shrewd idea where he was sailing to. A Board of Trade official arrived on board to change the ship's articles from coastal to foreign. A number of the crew requested not to make the trip, owing to sickness or family reasons, and were allowed to transfer ashore.

It is said that the crew that remained aboard were unhappy and some even talked of going on strike. After negotiations with representatives of the National Union of Seaman, the company offered an ex-gratis bonus payment of £30 for any inconvenience involved. The crew totalled just 398, compared to the normal peace time complement of 1,296.

The ship was under instructions to meet the King's Messenger, dispatched by the First Lord of the Admiralty, Winston Churchill, on 2 March, who delivered their sealed orders. Inside the envelope was the written order, 'Take her to New York with all speed'. After bunkering up and making adjustments to the compass, still affixed with portions of the launch gear attached to the hull, she set sail at 11 p.m. that evening. Underway at last, she slipped through the anti-submarine boom that stretched across the Clyde between Gantocks and Cloch Lighthouse, and headed west. She was escorted by Avo Anson aircraft and four Royal Navy destroyers as far as the Northern Irish coast before heading out alone into the Atlantic on a zigzag course at 27½ knots.

A calculated gamble was made that the *Queen Elizabeth* could outrun any lurking U-boat wolf packs. Speed and surprise would be her best defence. She was unarmed, other than pillboxes on the bridge and stern. Radio silence was ordered, but a communication was sent to her secret call sign, GBSS, to change course and avoid a convoy as a precaution against discovery. At night the entire ship was 'blacked out' and to aid this all windows and portholes had been painted over with anonymous matt battleship grey paint.

Meanwhile, in New York, Cunard's Percy Furness was briefing the New York office manager Robert Blake that he should be prepared to receive an unexpected visitor, the *Queen Elizabeth*. Blake smiled and responded, 'Hmm. That means we'll have to move the *Mauretania* from Pier 90 to make room for her'. On 6 March, Moran Towing Company tugs quietly transferred the *Mauretania*, but this did not go unnoticed by local reporters. Rumours began to circulate Manhattan that something big was approaching New York off Nantucket, heading towards the Ambrose. The suspicions were that it could be Cunard's *Queen Elizabeth*. Before first light on 7 March a Trans World Air Line aircraft took off, piloted by the vice-president of the airline and packed with reporters festooned with cameras and notebooks. Sure enough, they soon spotted a huge liner with two gigantic smoking funnels, but the only signs of life on board were two miniature figures waving up from the stern. The *New York Post* called her the '*Empress Incognito*'.

By the time she entered the Narrows at New York, news had spread all around the city that a great new British superliner was entering the harbour. Work stopped and people gazed down from the skyscrapers while others ran to welcome her from the shoreline. She paused at Quarantine and picked up the docking pilot, but by now the secret of her Atlantic dash was out.

Tugs of the Moran fleet carefully edged the *Queen Elizabeth* into her berth at Pier 90, alongside the three other superliners of the Atlantic. The quartet was to remain heavily guarded, for neutral New York was infested with German spies.

On 1 March the *Queen Mary* was 'called up', but she did not depart from New York until 21 March, bound for Sydney, Australia, where she was to be converted into a trooper capable of carrying 5,000 soldiers. Meanwhile, the *Queen Elizabeth* remained in New York for basic fitting out with completion of electrical wiring and lighting. The launch gear was removed and the bottom of the ship was refurbished, as by then she had been in the water for two years.

Towards the end of October additional crewmen arrived in New York, having travelled via Canada. The liner's complement was brought up to 465 and the *Queen Elizabeth* was replenished with fuel, water and supplies. The New York newspapers began to speculate that something was about to happen. She remained at New York until 3.30 p.m. on 13 November, when she slipped her berth. Her destination was Singapore where she would be extensively converted into His Majesty's Troop Ship *Queen Elizabeth*.

After the fall of France on 15 May 1940, the United States Treasury Department detailed 150 members of the US Coast Guard to go aboard the *Normandie*, still at Pier 88, to defend against possible German sabotage. On 1 November 1941 the US Coast Guard became part of the US Navy and on 12 December 1941, five days after the attack on Pearl Harbor, Captain Hervé Lehude and his French crew were removed. Eight days later, on 20 December 1941, the US Auxiliary Vessels Board officially approved the transfer of the *Normandie* to the US Navy for conversion to a troopship. She was renamed USS *Lafayette* in honour of the Marquis de la Fayette, the French general who fought on the Colonies' behalf in the American Revolution.

Serious consideration was given to proposals to convert the USS *Lafayette* into an aircraft carrier, but these were dropped in favour of conversion to a troop transport. The ship remained at Pier 88 and on the 27 December 1941 a contract was awarded to Robins Dry Dock & Repair Co. to undertake conversion work with an estimated completion date of 31 January 1942.

Captain Robert Coman reported as *Layfayette*'s prospective commanding officer on 31 January 1942, with command of a skeleton engineering force of 458 men. A week later, orders arrived that the *Layfayette* was to sail on

14 February. However, tragedy struck the liner at 2.30 p.m. on 9 February 1942, when sparks from a welding torch ignited a stack of life vests. These vests were filled with flammable kapok and had been stored in the former First Class Lounge. The small fire quickly spread to woodwork. Worse still the liner's very efficient fire protection system had been disconnected and the internal pumping system had been deactivated.

Approximately fifteen minutes after the fire had broken out, the New York City Fire Department arrived on the scene and immediately set about trying to tackle the blaze. To their horror, they discovered that their imperial measurement hoses were incompatible to the European metric measurement hoses and they were forced to try to fight the fire by manual means. Strong north-westerly winds blowing over the ship's port quarter swept the flames forward. Blinding black smoke now began to billow out of the ship, forcing fire fighters to pour on water from fireboats and on shore. The intake of water caused the great liner to list alarmingly.

The ship's designer, Vladimir Yourkevitch, arrived at the scene to offer his advice and expertise. At first the New York Harbor Police barred him from entry, although he begged them to allow him to assist. His suggestion was to open the sea cocks, thus flooding the lower decks and allowing the ship to settle on the seabed a few feet below. It would then be possible to pump water directly on to the burning areas without the risk of capsize. The Port Director, Admiral Andrews, rejected this suggestion. This resulted in the stricken liner listing to port. Water then entered through submerged openings, leading to eventual capsize at an angle of 80 degrees at 2.45 a.m. on 10 February.

Speculation in New York was that enemy sabotage was widely suspected, but an investigation concluded that the fire was completely accidental. Evidence was found that there was carelessness, rule violations during the poorly planned conversion of the ship and a clear lack of command structure during the fire.

The remains of the pride of the French Line were stripped and the hull was righted on 7 August 1943. On 15 September the hull was towed to dry dock with a view to restoration and conversion to an aircraft and transport ferry. An inspection revealed that the remains of the ship were beyond economic repair due to the extensive damage to the hull. She remained abandoned, decaying and rusting, until 3 October 1946, when she was sold for scrap to Lipsett Inc. at Port Newark, New Jersey.

When the United States entered the Second World War, the German High Command set up 'Operation Drumbeat', codenamed 'Operation Paukenschlag'. This was also known among the German submarine commanders as the 'American Shooting Season'. The German operation involved the U-boat aces of the Kriegsmarine targeting shipping departing and entering New York. The German U-boat commander, Vice Admiral Karl Donitz, noted that the standard Type VII U-Boat had insufficient range to patrol off the coast of New York. Therefore the larger Type IX U-boats, which were less manoeuvrable and slower to submerge, were selected for the assignment. The first five were deployed from Lorient in France on 18 December 1941, each carrying sealed orders to be opened after passing 20 degrees west. The Germans had no detailed navigation charts of New York Harbor. Kapitanleutnant Reihard Hardegen of the U-123 was only provided with two tourist guides of New York, one of which contained a fold-out map of the harbour.

On reaching the harbour, the U-boat captains were able to silhouette ships against the glow from the city lighting. In spite of US Navy patrols, the U-boats were able to attack within New York Harbor with relative impunity. The tanker *Coimbria* was torpedoed off Sandy Hook and the *Norness* off Long Island. This was a hard lesson for the United States to learn, but still local authorities resisted suggestions that they should follow the British-style total 'black-out' of lighting. Some lighting was, however, darkened in Coney Island, Brooklyn and the Sandy Hook Lighthouse. Anti-submarine nets were deployed and observers positioned along the Narrows.

The German U-boat offensive was known as the 'Second Happy Time' and lasted from January to August 1942. U-boat commanders perceived the defensive measures in New York Harbor as weak and disorganised. U-boats inflicted massive damage with little risk, resulting in 609 ships sunk, totalling 3.1 million tons for the loss of twenty-two U-boats.

As the war progressed defensive measures in New York Harbor radically improved. The use of aircraft to support US Navy destroyers began to have an effect on the Kriegsmarine U-boats and it was possible to transform New York Harbor into a busy assembly point for convoys to Europe and North Africa and this reached a peak in March 1943, when 543 ships were at anchor or berthed awaiting assignment. New York Harbor was the busiest port in the world with 39 active shipyards, 1,100 warehouses, 575 tugboats and 750 piers and docks, all devoted to the war effort. An endless supply of Liberty ships for convoys to Europe rolled off the shipyard production lines of Hoboken, New Jersey and Brooklyn. Many historians concluded that the contribution of New York Harbor turned the tide of the war in Europe.

Some 1,209 United States GIs, former prisoners of the Germans, are seen arriving in New York aboard the Swedish SS *Gripsholm* on 21 February 1945. The gleaming white *Gripsholm* was clearly marked, in big bold letters, 'diplomat', in order to distinguish her as a 'neutral ship'. *Associated Press*

Left: A focused close-up view of the enormous anchors on the stern and bow of the French Line *Normandie* at Pier 88 in July 1938. Note the huge, gold-coloured letters of its name. *Britton Collection*

Below: Disaster! The former French Line *Normandie*, now renamed USS *Lafayette*, is pictured ablaze on 9 February 1942. Firefighters are pictured on shore and on fireboats, pouring water onto the fire. The inferno eventually caused the great liner to capsize at 2.45 the following morning. *Associated Press*

The Cunard RMS *Queen Mary* painted in Admiralty camouflage grey sets sail from New York on 21 March 1940, shrouded in upmost secrecy. *Associated Press*

Passengers and crew on the French Line *Normandie* peer down to watch provisions for the voyage ahead being loaded aboard via the open starboard shell door at Pier 88 in July 1938. *Britton Collection*

In the thirty-six hours preceding this remarkable aerial picture, taken on 16 September 1941, 104 ships eased into New York Harbor. Viewed from Staten Island looking towards Bay Ridge, Brooklyn, they included fifty-three British, Dutch and Norwegian vessels, many of them tankers. After loading, the convoy sailed to Britain with vital war supplies. *Associated Press*

Looking down on a convoy sailing from New York to Britain packed with vital war supplies on 5 November 1941. *Associated Press*

Post-War Years 1945–80

Straight after the Second World War, in 1946, New York Harbor was hit by a seven-day tug strike of the 3,500 crewmembers. With potential food shortages in New York and much discontent, the New York Marine Towing & Transportation Employers Association gave way to the strikers' demands for better working conditions, including a thirty-hour week and a basic rate of pay of $2.96 for deck hands and $4.04 for captains.

The year 1946 also saw the return from Europe of entire divisions of US forces aboard the Cunard RMS *Queen Mary* and RMS *Queen Elizabeth*. On other voyages, these liners carried across the Atlantic into New York GI brides and their families from Europe. Jurisdiction over the city airports was also transferred to the New York & New Jersey Port Authority in 1946.

For many years serious consideration had been given to linking the boroughs of Staten Island and Brooklyn in New York City at the Narrows. In 1929 there was much debate about the construction of a tunnel at this point, but preliminary studies had been firstly halted by the Depression and later the Second World War. In 1945 the tunnel idea was again revived. However, an option to construct a bridge received greater support, as it would cost less to build and maintain, could be constructed faster and would have greater traffic capacity. The military authorities were concerned with the proposal to build a bridge over the Narrows on the grounds that the destruction of a bridge could potentially trap their naval vessels based in New York Harbor. After some debate, the New York State Legislature decided to authorise the construction of a bridge, as they considered that the development of nuclear weapons made senseless any opposition to the bridge.

Early in 1954 specialists began making test borings for the bridge piers, ready for construction to commence on 13 August 1959. The naming of the bridge sparked off hot debate. In 1951, when the bridge was at the planning stage, the Italian Historical Society of America proposed to name the completed bridge the Verrazano Bridge, after the Florentine explorer Giovanni da Verrazzano. Robert Moses, the New York State Parks Commissioner, turned down this initial proposal. The society responded by launching a public relations campaign to promote the idea of naming the bridge after Verrazzano, followed by a second approach to the Bridge and Tunnel Authority, but the proposal was again turned down. The manager of the authority backed Robert Moses' original decision, stating that the name was too long and that he had never heard of Verrazzano.

The Italian Historical Society of America next lobbied the New York State Assembly to present a bill that would name the bridge after the explorer. When the bill was presented to the Assembly, the Staten Island Chamber of Commerce declared their support for the society in promoting the name. The bill was signed into law in 1960 by Governor Nelson Rockefeller. The debate over the name of the bridge appeared to have been settled, but when President John F. Kennedy was assassinated, a petition was raised with thousands of signatures to name the bridge the Kennedy Bridge. In response, the late president's brother, US Attorney General Robert Kennedy, requested that New York's international airport be renamed John F. Kennedy Airport instead and the bridge keep its intended name.

The upper deck of the bridge was opened by New York City Mayor Robert F. Wagner on 21 November 1964 and named the Verrazano-Narrows Bridge. Wagner was the first person to officially drive over the bridge, but the lower deck did not open until 28 June 1969. The construction came to $320 million and sadly three men died building the bridge. At the time of its completion, the new bridge was the longest suspension bridge in the world. Each of the two towers contains 1 million bolts and 3 million rivets. The diameter of each of the four suspension cables is 36 inches and each of the cables is composed of 26,108 wires, amounting to 143,000 miles in length.

The entry into service of the SS *United States* at New York on 4 July 1952 will forever be the port's proudest day. This national icon was constructed between 1950 to 1952 at the Newport News Shipbuilding and Drydock Company in Newport News, Virginia. Prior to her maiden voyage, the people of New York were able to inspect the great liner and gaze in awe and wonder. On the maiden voyage the SS *United States* broke the transatlantic speed record, previously held by the Cunard RMS *Queen Mary*, by ten hours. Remarkably she crossed the Atlantic from the Ambrose Lightship at New York Harbor to Bishop's Rock off Cornwall in Britain in three days, ten hours and forty minutes, at an average speed of 35.59 knots. This outstanding ocean liner also broke the return westbound crossing record by completing the voyage to New York in three days, twelve hours and twelve minutes at an average speed of 34.51 knots. In so doing the SS *United States* obtained the Blue Riband accolade, given to the passenger liner crossing the Atlantic in the fastest time, and was awarded the Hales Trophy. On her triumphant return to New York the whole city appeared to line the shores of New York Harbor and the deafening salutes from the whistles of the accompanying armada of tugs, pleasure craft and shipping which joined her from the Narrows has never been repeated. New York was rightfully proud of their great ship as she tied up at Pier 86, a national hero and the envy of the world.

The post-war period into the early 1960s was the boom time transatlantic passenger travel on the ocean liners and thus for New York Harbor. The Port of New York had eighteen active passenger piers or a total of thirty-six separate berths along its waterfront. On the Jersey side of the Hudson River there was the Harbourside Terminal in downtown Jersey City, with the largest cold-storage warehouse in the world. Further north, at Hoboken Port Authority Piers, was the home of American Export Line combo liners. Two blocks further down, Holland America Line used two piers for its seven liners and six auxiliary passenger ships.

In Brooklyn troop transports of the Military Sea Transportation Service used the gigantic Army Terminal at 58th Street, catering for servicemen and their families. It consisted of vast office and warehouse spaces in addition to four 1,500ft-long piers. The future looked very bright for the post-war New York Harbor, but this was all to change.

The advent of the jet age in the late 1950s and early 1960s, with the introduction of the British De Havilland Comet and US Boeing 707 aircraft, revolutionised transatlantic travel and had a profound impact on New York Harbor. Despite the introduction of superb new liners, like the SS *United States* and the *France*, passenger numbers dropped dramatically. Often there were more staff members on board than fare-paying passengers. By the mid-1970s, New York was basically a cruise port for ships heading south to Bermuda, the Bahamas and Caribbean. Royalty and film stars now preferred to travel by air. Rocketing fuel costs and wages for labour added to the depression of New York Harbor. It was now almost impossible to purchase a ticket on an ocean liner to Europe, as shipping lines abandoned their facilities in New York and pulled out. Even the cruise liners started to call into New York more infrequently as cruises began to start at Miami, Port Everglades and San Juan, which had quick inexpensive air connection transfers. Passengers seeking rest and enjoyment no longer wished to commence their cruises at New York with a coldish voyage south to the Caribbean.

The response of the Port Authority was to mothball, close and frequently demolish pier and berthing facilities. In 1963 Pier 40 was revamped with a quite revolutionary facility which offered three passenger-ship berths. In 1974 this facility was closed, when reduced sailings caused the transfer and concentration of operations to the mid-town Passenger Ship Terminal. In 1973 a $35 million facelift was given to Piers 88, 90 and 92. This re-development included the fitting of air-conditioning for the summer months and heating for the winter time. When work was completed in November 1974 all other passenger ship piers were closed and boarded up. The once-prestigious piers began to decay rapidly and suffered from erosion from the Hudson. Sadly, vandals attacked some of the neglected piers and set fire to them. Cranes then moved in to demolish the scorched and rusting remains. Even the once-proud Holland America Line Terminal on the opposite side of the Hudson at Hoboken met the same fate. Almost overnight the Chelsea Piers disappeared at the hands of a single demolition crane equipped with a steel ball.

It was not just the passenger facilities that changed in New York Harbor; the shipping of freight fundamentally changed too, as the Port of New York and New Jersey was forced to adapt to the container revolution. Loose cargo shipping began to rapidly decline as more and more freight was shipped by container. New York Harbor rebuilt facilities to become the third largest container port in the USA. It has also become the largest oil importing port in the nation and can accommodate the largest super-tankers. The port has diminished in importance to passenger travel, but has adapted to change and has a bright commercial future.

The 35,739-ton Cunard RMS *Mauretania* has been camouflaged in Admiralty grey and is seen being prepared for sailing from New York at 8 p.m. on 20 March 1940. *Associated Press*

Packed with 1,719 war brides of American servicemen and 615 children, the Cunard RMS *Queen Mary* gently docks in New York on 12 February 1945. *Associated Press*

Left: An entire division of 14,000 American GIs return to their home shores in New York aboard the Cunard RMS *Queen Mary* on 20 June 1945, following action in Europe. *Associated Press*

Below: This original unique Photorama wide-angle negative shows the triumphant United States Line SS *United States* at Pier 86 just after she completed her record-winning crossing of the Atlantic in 1952. *Photorama original negative/Britton Collection*

The *PROUD* NEW HOLDER of the ATLANTIC BLUE RIBBON SPEED RECORD.

photorama L.Azarraga

The unprecedented welcome to New York of the United States Line SS *United States*, escorted by a flotilla of boats and helicopters overhead on 23 June 1952. *Associated Press*

The Holland America Line's 758ft-long SS *Nieuw Amsterdam* is almost perfectly framed by the gigantic Verrazano-Narrows Bridge. *Britton Collection*

UNITED STATES LINES COMPANY

ONE BROADWAY

NEW YORK 4, N. Y.

OFFICE OF
VICE PRESIDENT

TELEPHONE
(212) DI 4-5800

November 21, 1964

On this special occasion ...

It is a particular pleasure to send you this collector's item - FIRST DAY OF ISSUE of the Verrazano-Narrows Bridge stamp. Such a commemorative stamp is issued by official Act of Congress, and whether a stamp buff or not we hope you find this of historic interest.

By a unique coincidence the SS UNITED STATES passed directly beneath the bridge during opening day ceremonies. Those present were reminded of the contrast between the small, frail carrack on which Verrazano entered New York Bay, and the magnificent 53,000 ton superliner - the largest, fastest, and most modern vessel ever built in America.

Actually the SS UNITED STATES was returning from dry dock in Virginia to her Pier completely refurbished to prepare to sail this Wednesday on a cruise to Bermuda with a capacity list of almost a thousand passengers.

We therefore also take this opportunity to thank you for this outstanding example of your wonderful support which contributes so much to the success of the SS UNITED STATES on her trans-Atlantic run and cruises.

It is our hope that in the future you will continue to have many of your clients view the world's longest suspension bridge at the gateway of New York from the broad and spacious decks of the superliner UNITED STATES.

Sincerely,

Kenneth F Gautier

K. F. Gautier
Vice President-Passenger Traffic

KFG:hg

Verrazano-Narrows Bridge: The SS *United States'* first-day cover letter.

A deck view on board the Hamburg Atlantic Line SS *Hanseatic* looking forwards past the gigantic red funnels as the inbound liner approaches the Ambrose Lightship in May 1962. She was originally built as the three-funnel *Empress of Scotland* but was refitted and converted to emerge as the twin-funnel *Hanseatic*. On 8 September 1966, the ship caught fire whilst at berth in New York. The fire spread from the engine room and gutted five decks. Subsequently *Hanseatic* was scrapped after being declared uneconomic to repair. *Britton Collection*

A final opportunity to sunbathe at the stern of the TS *Bremen* before docking at New York in 1970. *Britton Collection*

Left: The Ambrose Lightship and The Narrows entrance to New York Harbor are spotted dead ahead by the navigation officer on the American Export Line SS *Independence* on 8 June 1954. *Britton Collection*

Below: The Ambrose Lightship, officially known as USCG *Lightship 613*, is pictured just off the starboard side of Cunard RMS *Queen Elizabeth*. Sailors on the Atlantic liners have often considered the Ambrose Lightship as the outer marker of New York Harbor. This lightship was retired in 1967 and replaced by an unmanned oil rig-type structure with a 6-million candlepower light that flashes every 7½ seconds. *Arthur Oakman/Britton Collection*

Right: Looking through the Shell Door, we can see that the *Queen Elizabeth* has slowed as the Sandy Hook pilot boat approaches in 1953. *Arthur Oakman/ Britton Collection*

Below: Having scrambled up the Jacob's ladder to the open Shell Door, the Sandy Hook pilot is silhouetted as he boards the *Queen Elizabeth*. *Arthur Oakman/Britton Collection*

The United States Line Blue Riband record-holding SS *United States* has slowed down after crossing the Atlantic to take on a Sandy Hook pilot who will navigate a safe course into New York. A miniature US Coast Guard vessel is pictured at the top of the image, escorting the superliner. *World Ship Society*

Plans for the new Verrazano-Narrows Bridge are unveiled at an open-air meeting with an excited crowd on 13 August 1959. *Britton Collection*

Above: Known to all British shipping enthusiasts as the 'Great White Whale', the 44,000-ton P&O Line cruise liner SS *Canberra* is pictured sailing towards the Verrazano-Narrows Bridge, which is under construction. She was built for the Southampton–Australia service, but was pictured visiting New York as part of the 'Visit America' cruise, having berthed at Pier 92 for two nights to allow the 2,200 passengers to explore the city of New York and savour some of the great shows on Broadway. *Britton Collection*

Right: Approaching the Verrazano-Narrows Bridge when sailing in and out of New York Harbor is always a very exciting occasion. In this view we can see the bridge ahead, looking forwards from the bridge of the Cunard RMS *Sylvania* in August 1965. *Britton Collection*

Left: Passengers gaze up in awe and wonder at the Verrazano-Narrows Bridge from the deck of the outbound Cunard RMS *Sylvania* as an inbound United Fruit Line vessel passes in the opposite direction in August 1965. *Britton Collection*

Below: Opened on 21 November 1964, the Verrazano Narrows Bridge carries twelve roadways on six upper and six lower lanes. This double-decked suspension bridge connects the boroughs of Staten Island and Brooklyn at the Narrows. *Britton Collection*

Left: A close-up view of the bridge and aft decks of the 41,900-ton P&O *Oriana*, not a regular visitor to New York, as she passes under the Verrazano Narrows Bridge. She was on a three-week 'Voyage to the New World' cruise from Southampton, which included a three-day stay at Pier 88 in New York. *Britton Collection*

Below: In 1963, Moore-McCormack Lines rebuilt the superstructure of their 613ft SS *Brasil*, which is pictured here sailing under the Verrazano Narrows Bridge on 3 February 1966. This delightful ship went on to be renamed as *Volendam*, *Monarch Sun*, *Island Sun*, *Liberté*, *Canada Star*, *Queen of Bermuda*, *Enchanted Sea* and *Universe Explorer*. *Britton Collection*

After being sold by the United States Line to the Chandris Line in 1964, the SS *America* was renamed SS *Australis* until 1978, when she was purchased by Venture Cruises and reverted to her previous identity as SS *America*. Here she is seen with the Verrazano Narrows Bridge in the background on 1 July 1978. The *America* set sail on her first Venture Cruises voyage on 30 June 1978, but her refit had not been completed by the time of sailing. The ship was filthy, with piles of soiled linen, worn mattresses and litter. Passengers described the stench of engine oil, sewage, and generally unsavoury smells throughout the liner. Water was also said to be leaking from pipes in cabins and on the decks. Due to overbooking, the situation on board became intolerable and the passengers mutinied, forcing the captain to return to New York, as shown in this picture. Upon arriving back in New York 960 passengers were offloaded, and after her second sailing an additional 200 passengers also decided to leave the ship via a tender at Staten Island. The outcome of this cruise to Nova Scotia was $2.5 million worth of passenger claims. *Britton Collection*

The colossal 151ft-high neoclassical sculpture *Statue of Liberty* as seen through the port hole of the Cunard RMS *Queen Elizabeth* in August 1963. It was designed by Frederic Bartholdi and was a gift to the United States from the people of France. The robed female figure represents the Roman goddess Libertas and she bears a torch and a tablet evoking the law. The statue is a national icon of the United States of America representing freedom. It was and still is a welcoming beacon to all immigrants arriving in New York. *Britton Collection*

The doomed flagship of the Italian Line, *Andrea Doria*, sails past Manhattan and towards the open Atlantic, next stop Gibraltar. She was to meet her fate on 25 July 1956 after a collision off Nantucket with the Swedish liner *Stockholm*. This accident resulted in severe loss of life and the sinking of this magnificent 29,000-ton Italian liner. *Richard Faber/ Britton Collection*

This original painting hung in the Cunard office at New York until November 1965. It was used by Cunard for publicity and advertising. When the ship was withdrawn from service the painting was removed from public display, wrapped in brown paper tied with string and lay forgotten and unseen for forty-seven years until rescued by the author! *Britton Collection*

La bannière étoilée des Etats-Unis et la reine de la flotte française, le Liberté. The stars and stripes flag of the United States of America proudly flutters in the breeze from the stern of a Moran tugboat as the beautiful French Line SS *Liberté* gently sails past bound for Le Havre and Europe on 21 March 1959. *Britton Collection*

Left: 'Operation Sail' in 1976 was the celebration of the United States bicentennial, the 200th anniversary of the adoption of the United States Declaration of Independence. Sixteen sailing ships sailed into New York to participate in the parade of ships. Each sailing ship flew a banner featuring a tricolour star insignia of the bicentennial. In this picture, two Moran Towing Co. tugboats escort a sailing vessel into New York in preparation for the celebrations. *F.J. Duffy, Moran Towing/Britton Collection*

Below: It was as if the whole city of New York turned out to witness the spectacle of 'Operation Sail' to celebrate the bicentennial in 1976. The US Navy was also present to join in the celebrations with an aircraft carrier and guided missile destroyer. *Mac Owen/ Britton Collection*

Left: Piers 57 and 58, West Street, with a Grace Line Santa Class ship berthed ready for unloading. In the background is the imposing 102-storey Empire State Building on the intersection of Fifth Avenue and West 34th Street. It has a roof height of 1,250ft but, with its antenna spire included, it stands at 1,454ft high. *Britton Collection*

Above: A brace of cruise ships sail from New York, the 18,017-ton Chandris Line SS *Britanis* sailing to Bermuda with 1,200 passengers and the Home Lines 39,241-ton SS *Oceanic* sailing to Nassau on a seven-day cruise, ably assisted by Moran tugboats. *Jim Gavin*

Left: The Cunard RMS *Queen Mary* bids *au revoir* to New York, with her paying off pennant proudly fluttering in the breeze as a flotilla of Moran Towing tugboats escort her down the Hudson for the final time on 22 September 1967. *Marc Piche*

Left: The gigantic twin funnels of the Chandris Line SS *Britanis* are pictured from the flying bridge of the liner. The SS *Britanis* was built in 1931 and began her maiden voyage on the 3 June 1932, sailing for Matson Lines as the SS *Montery*. She saw active war service, with the name USAT *Montery*, as a fast troop carrier in the Pacific and on the North Atlantic, conveying up to 6,000 troops per voyage. She ended her distinguished passenger service in 1996 and was sold for scrap in July 2000, but on her final voyage to the Indian scrap yard she broke free of the tugboat towing her and sank 50 miles off Cape Town in South Africa on 21 October 2000. *Britton Collection*

Above: Photographer Jim Gavin has captured a dramatically smoky scene through his lens as the SS *Oceanic*, with passengers lining the decks, sails down the Hudson. *Jim Gavin*

Above: Crowds line the shores as the brand-new United States Line SS *United States* sails past the Battery on her record-breaking maiden voyage to Europe to win the Blue Riband in July 1952. *Britton Collection*

Right: The Cunard *Queen Elizabeth 2* (*QE2*) completes her maiden-voyage arrival at New York into Pier 90 with the assistance of three Moran tugs on her port bow. *Britton Collection*

Left: An aerial view of Luxury Liner Row in October 1967, with, from left to right, the Day Liner steamer *Alexander Hamilton*, Home Line *Oceanic*, an unidentified United States Line freighter, the North German Lloyd TS *Bremen*, the twin-funnelled Italian Line *Michelangelo* and the Cunard RMS *Franconia*. *Britton Collection*

Left: Cheering crowds wave their final farewells from Pier 84 at West 44th Street to passengers on the departing American Export Line SS *Constitution* on 8 June 1954. Note the party of nuns of Our Lady St Mary the Virgin pictured on the right-hand side of the picture. Could one of their order have been making a pilgrimage on board the SS *Constitution* to hear Pope Pius XII at the Vatican in Rome? The year 1954 in the Catholic Church was a Marian year for the centennial of the Dogma of the Immaculate Conception. *Britton Collection*

Below: An extraordinary picture, taken in the middle of the Hudson River on board the 23,719-ton American Export Line's SS *Constitution* on 8 June 1954. Just take a second look at the period clothing, with the ladies' hats and smartly dressed gentlemen in their suits. Note the brace of Lackwanna steam ferries on the river and the two sister ferries docked in the Lackwanna Railroad Ferry Terminal; also the Moran tugboat. *Britton Collection*

The quayside looks extremely busy at Pier 84 with a variety of vintage lorries assisting with the unloading of passenger luggage and trunks from the American Export Line's SS *Independence*. *Britton Collection*

A glorious view of the American Export Line's SS *Independence* in the North River on 20 January 1968. In 1959, the *Independence* and the *Constitution* were rebuilt. The bridge wings and navigation rooms were repositioned 21ft forward and elevated by 8½ft, and additional passenger accommodation was added. During the annual refit at Todds Shipyard the following year, both liners emerged in a pleasing new all-white livery. *Braun Brothers/Britton Collection*

A close-up view of the bow and anchors of the American Export Line's SS *Independence* looking resplendent in her all-white post-1960 livery in October 1967. *Britton Collection*

Left: Pier 84, West 44th Street, noticeboard. The notice refers to the sailing of the Italian Line liner *Michelangelo* at 12.00 p.m. on 8 March 1966 from Pier 84. *Britton Collection*

Below: Heading up the Hudson River in June 1969 to Pier 84, West 44th Street, is the 761ft-long Italian Line SS *Leonardo da Vinci.* She was repainted in all-white livery in 1965. *Britton Collection*

½ MICHELANGELO
WILL SAIL
12 NOON   MAR. 8

Left: The ill-fated Italian Line *Andrea Doria* is seen in happier times at Pier 84, West 44th Street, and is receiving some touching up painting to her anchor and chains. *Britton Collection*

Below: The funnel and top deck of the Italian Line *Leonardo da Vinci* peep over the top of Pier 84 in March 1966. *Britton Collection*

Right: This picture shows a typical busy scene at the entrance to Pier 84, West 44th Street, with the United States Line liners SS *America* and SS *United States* pictured berthed at the adjacent Pier 86. The New York cop has his work cut out marshalling cars and yellow cabs, which are dropping off passengers for the 12.00 p.m. departure of the American Export Line *Constitution*. All that is missing from this picture is the noise of shouting, the chattering of excited passengers, the peep of car horns and the smell from the hot burger stand just out of picture on the left! *Britton Collection*

Below: This spectacular view of the SS *United States* sailing to Europe was taken from Weehawken looking across the Hudson River towards Pier 86, West 46th Street, home of the United States Line. To the left of the stars and stripes flag of the United States is the Alexander Hamilton monument, which commemorates the famous duel of 12 July 1804 in which he was killed. Alexander Hamilton is pictured on the United States $10 bill. *Britton Collection*

A water-level shot of the mooring ropes and United States Line portable gangways that criss-cross this picture at Pier 86 on West 44th Street. The SS *America* arrived just minutes before from Le Havre, France, and her passengers are rushing ashore to claim their baggage at the customs check in. *Britton Collection*

Perhaps the most famous ocean-liner funnels in New York were those of the SS *United States*. With the liner safely berthed at Pier 86, some members of the crew saunter along the deck past the lifeboats and those gigantic red funnels. *Britton Collection*

AROUND THE PORT

Chelsea Piers

As with many maritime families, the Chelsea Piers hold a special memory for the Britton family, for it was here that the author's grandfather stepped ashore in the United States off a White Star luxury liner from Southampton. Even before the piers were opened in 1910, the first new British luxury liners *Lusitania* and *Mauretania* docked at the Chelsea Piers. Designed by the architectural firm of Warren & Wetmore, which also designed Grand Central Station, the Chelsea Piers replaced a conglomerate of run-down waterfront structures. When opened the piers looked magnificent with a row of grand buildings embellished with pink granite façades.

In the 1910s, my grandfather's day, the Chelsea Piers welcomed the famed ocean liners from Europe. On occasions the air would be filled with clouds of acrid black smoke belching from twenty funnels as five four-funnel liners prepared to sail down the Hudson on the incoming tide. To the shipping enthusiast this must have made a spectacular sight. At the same time as the rich and famous were arriving at the Chelsea Piers so too were many poor immigrants who had travelled across the Atlantic in overcrowded steerage class. The piers were bustling with activity and this was their heyday as celebrities posed for press pictures and interviews when travelling in grand style to or from Europe.

The Chelsea Piers served the needs of the Port of New York first as a passenger ship terminal, then as an embarkation point for soldiers sailing to the battlefields of Europe in the First and Second World Wars. In the 1930s, however, huge new ocean liners like the Cunard RMS *Queen Mary* and French Line *Normandie* came steaming into New York, sweeping the Chelsea Piers into the past as new piers were built between West 44th and West 52nd Streets to cater for these new liners.

Busy waterfront on 7 April 1959 as the Cunard RMS *Mauretania* is manoeuvred into the Hudson by Moran tugs. Meanwhile, six ocean liners are seen berthed. From left to right: Cunard Line SS *Media*, RMS *Queen Mary* and *Ivernia*; French Line SS *Liberté*, United States Line SS *United States* and Italian Line *Giulio Cesare*. *Associated Press*

The French Line SS *Ile de France* sails past the Statue of Liberty and out through the Narrows, next stop Le Havre. *Britton Collection*

Perhaps the Chelsea Piers' final spotlight in front of the world's press came in July 1936, when the US Olympic team sailed to Berlin, Germany. The returning Olympic gold medal winner Jesse Owens was greeted as a national hero at the Chelsea Piers by excited crowds of cheering fans.

After the Second World War in the 1950s and '60s the piers changed their purpose to become a cargo terminal. Many shipping lines began to relocate to New Jersey and elsewhere in the port. From the mid-1960s, the Chelsea Piers became rather neglected and rundown, made obsolete by the advent of jet aircraft travel and the age of the container ship.

The four surviving Chelsea Piers have since been redeveloped for use as recreation centres and waterfront public use.

Luxury Liner Row

The Passenger Ship Terminals on the Hudson River between West 44th and West 57th streets are known to many as Luxury Liner Row. Until 1936, Cunard's main passenger terminal in New York was at the Chelsea Piers: 53, 54 and 56, which were located between West 13th and West 15th Streets. With the introduction into service of the new RMS *Queen Mary*, which was too long for the Chelsea Piers, Cunard used the specially built Pier 90. The smaller Cunard vessels continued to use the Chelsea Piers until the early 1950s.

Pier 25, Franklin Street, Argentine State Line

Argentina was the only South American country to operate ocean liners from New York, between 1951 and 1963. Its liners – *Rio de la Planta*, *Rio Jachal* and *Rio Tunuyan* – were instantly recognisable with their black funnels that had a blue band with white edges and a white anchor. It operated a forty-three-day round trip service from Pier 25 at New York to Buenos Aires via Rio de Janeiro, Santos and Montevideo, but returning via the same ports plus Trinidad and La Guaira (Caracas). The Argentine State

Line liners were of moderate size and speed, measuring 11,000 tons with spacious facilities to accommodate 116 passengers, all first class, which were designed to compete with the Moore-McCormack Lines' ships. The Argentine air-conditioned ships included staterooms with private or semi-private bath, a main lounge, smoke room bar, library, dining room and a tiled swimming pool and lido.

A family member who once had to travel from New York to Rio recalled that these liners were full of Latin American warmth and hospitality: 'The ship was full of loud Argentinean music and colourful, exotic Latin dancing ladies! There was a constant supply of alcohol with strong South American Quilmes beer followed by Aquardiente [firewater] made from sugar cane, making the voyage from New York a memorable occasion.'

Pier 32, Canal Street, Moore-McCormack Lines

Known to many in New York as simply, 'Mor-Mac', the Moore-McCormack Lines was a series of companies operating as shipping lines under the umbrella of the Moore-McCormack Company. Founded in 1913 in New York, Mor-Mac had its offices at 5 Broadway. The company operated

three ships – *Argentinia*, *Brazil* and the *Uruguay* – providing luxury accommodation for 550 passengers per ship from Pier 32 to the east coast of South America. The ships could be identified by the red letter 'M' set on a white disc, which was painted on a green band between the buff yellow and black top on the funnel. In 1957 Moore-McCormack acquired the Robin Line and added to its services from New York to African ports.

From 1956 Moore-McCormack began a vessel replacement program with fourteen new ships delivered by 1965. From the mid-1960s the company decided on a new replacement policy for a different type of vessel, realising that container traffic was the way to economic success for the future of shipping from New York. In the final years the Mor-Mac ships docked at Pier 97, West 57th Street. Moore-McCormack began to withdraw from the contracting passenger liner market and sold *Argentina* and *Brazil* to Holland America Line for conversion to cruising in 1972. After refit and conversion the ships re-emerged as Holland America's *Veendam* and *Volendam*. The McLean Lines bought out Moore-McCormack in December 1982.

Pier 32, Canal Street, Zim Lines

At the end of the Second World War the Jewish Agency and the General Federation of Labourers of Israel founded Zim Lines. Its first ship, the SS *Kedmah*, was not purchased until 1947 and she was used to transport thousands of migrants to the newly formed the state of Israel. The company added to its fleet by purchasing more ships – *Negba*, *Artza* and *Galila* – which helped supply food and military equipment to Israel. The growing fleet was increased by a further thirty-six ships following a reparations agreement with West Germany in 1953. The acquisition of the *Zion* and *Israel* in 1956 and the completion of the liner SS *Shalom* in 1964 saw regular services from New York to Haifa operate initially from Pier 64 in Manhattan before transferring to Pier 32, Canal Street. Zim Lines ships could always be picked out by their white funnels with seven yellow stars set between narrow blue bands.

On 26 November 1964, the *Shalom* accidentally collided with the Norwegian tanker *Stolt Dagali* just outside New York. Sadly this resulted in the loss of nineteen crew members of the Norwegian tanker as well as the stern of the *Stolt Dagali*.

Zim Lines' passenger services from New York only lasted until 1967 and the *Shalom* was sold to the German Atlantic Line, becoming its second SS *Hanseatic*.

Gala weekend on the waterfront at the Atlantic Terminal piers on 29 May 1962. Pulling out of Pier 90 is the Cunard RMS *Queen Mary* bound for Cherbourg and Southampton. Also pictured are, from bottom to top: American Export Line SS *Constitution*, United States Line SS *America* and SS *United States*, North German Lloyd TS *Bremen*, Cunard *Sylvania* and Moore-McCormack *Brasil*. *Associatied Press*

Pier 40, Houston Street, Holland America Line

Pier 40 was opened in 1963, after several piers were filled-in, and was at the time the most modern passenger facility on the New York waterfront. It was located across the street from the terminus of the High Line Railroad. Pier 40 was quite a revolutionary square-shape design and could offer three passenger-ship berths with an inner core vehicle parking facility.

Holland America Line transferred across the Hudson River from its base at Hoboken to the new facilities at Pier 40 and became the principal tenant. This was only to last just over a decade as in November 1974 the pier closed when the Port Authority mid-town Passenger Ship Terminal opened. After closure, Pier 40 became a storage facility and long-stay car park. At the time of writing Pier 40 remains in use as an indoor/outdoor athletics and football training facility.

Pier 42, Morton Street, Norwegian America Line

Founded in 1910, the Norwegian American Line ran regular transatlantic services between Norway, Denmark and New York. The aim of the company was to maintain a mail, cargo and passenger route, taking advantage of the immigrant trade, with ships named after Norwegian fjords. The ships' funnels of the Norwegian American Line were bright yellow with a blue band bordered by white and red bands.

With the decline in transatlantic passenger service, the Norwegian American Line ships began cruising, but by 1968 services to/from Oslo were in terminal decline and the transatlantic voyages were completely discontinued in 1971. The *Stavangerfjord* was retired and scrapped in 1963. The *Oslofjord* was chartered out for cruising to Costa Line, Italy, and renamed the *Fulvia*, but caught fire and sank off Tenerife in 1970. The *Bergensfjord*, which was built in 1956, was sold to the French Line in 1971 and renamed *De Grasse*. Norwegian America Line's two remaining ships, *Sagafjord* and *Vistafjord*, were sold to Cunard. By 1983 no ships were owned by Norwegian America Line and it is now a worldwide car-carrying company, using chartered vessels. Only memories of its great ships sailing into Pier 42 at New York remain.

Pier 57 and 58, West Street, Grace Line

In the late 1950s and early 1960s there were at least three Grace Line sailings every Friday from New York to South America and the Caribbean.

Its ships had distinctive green funnels with a white band and black top. The first Grace Line ships to sail from New York to the west coast of South America were sailing ships which had to round the treacherous Cape Horn and took 100 days to complete the voyage. Following the opening of the Panama Canal and the introduction of steam boats, the length of voyages was reduced considerably, to less than a month.

Grace Line was established as a commercial and shipping business in Callao, the port of Lima, Peru in the mid-1800s by two Irish-born brothers, William Russell and Michael. It began exporting fertilizer to the United States and in 1865 William established the firm of W.R. Grace in New York. He settled in the city and was twice elected Mayor of New York in 1880. In the 1890s the company expanded into the steamship freighter business operating from New York to the west coast of South America. At first the shipping line ran under the British flag, but from 1912 it sailed under the US flag and specialised in traffic to the west coast of South America before expanding with services to the Caribbean.

With the introduction of passenger services from New York to the ports on the west coast of South America in 1916, Grace Line contracted New York Shipping and Cramp to build five new ships: *Santa Ana*, *Santa Luisa*, *Santa Teresa*, *Santa Elisa* and *Santa Leonora*. These 5,800-ton passenger ships were 376ft long and had a service speed of 13 knots.

To comply with its mail contracts, Grace Line agreed to commission four new ships. Between 1932 and 1933, Grace Line commissioned the construction at the Federal Shipbuilding Yards at Kearney in New York Harbor of four Santa Rosa Class liners: *Santa Elena*, *Santa Lucia*, *Santa Paula* and *Santa Rosa*. They were designed by William Francis Gibbs, who was later to achieve fame as the designer of the record-breaking SS *United States*. The quartet of new Santa Rosa Class ships established the first passenger service between New York and Seattle. At first the service made a call at Philadelphia, but from 1934 this was withdrawn. The time saved in the sailing schedule meant ships were able to make a shuttle between Seattle and San Francisco. In the following years further Santa liners were constructed and entered service into the Grace Line fleet.

Grace Line shipping sailing from New York was hit hard during the Second World War. The US Navy took over the *Santa Lucia* in 1942 and renamed her as the USS *Leedstown*. Sadly she was sunk in the North African invasion. The *Santa Elena* was also sunk the following year off Philippville, on the Algerian coast. The invasion of Normandy in June 1944 accounted for further losses with the *Santa Clara* and the *Susan B Anthony* both going down. Of the Grace Line ships built for operation

Grace Line ticket from New York.

from New York before 1939 only the *Santa Rosa* and *Santa Paula* survived, but their commitment to the 'war effort' rendered them in a rundown state, requiring major refits and refurbishment. Both ships continued to be flagships of the Grace Line fleet, operating out of New York until 1958 when they were replaced by new Gibbs & Cox designed ships of the same name. The new 584ft-long ships were 15,000 tons and proved a welcome modern addition to the Grace Line fleet, operating from Piers 57 and 58, West Street, New York.

In 1968 the 15th Street Grace Line Terminal was closed and services were transferred to Holland America Line's Pier 40. The following year Grace Line was sold to Prudential Line and she operated under the name of Prudential Grace Line. However, a year later Prudential decided to suspend the Caribbean service and the *Santa Rosa* and *Santa Paula* were laid up. At its peak, Grace Line was a major shipping force in New York Harbor with twenty-three ships totalling 188,000 tons.

Pier 64 West, 24th Street, Panama Steamship Line

The Panama Steamship Line used Pier 64 up until 1961, conveying passengers, mail and cargo from New York to Panama. The three Bethlehem Steel-built cargo liners which belonged to the line – *Ancon*, *Cristobal* and *Panama* – would sail in rotation at 4 p.m. on either Tuesdays or Fridays. The funnels of the ships were painted yellow with three aluminium bands. In 1957 the fleet was slimmed down when the *Panama* was sold to American President Lines and renamed *President Hoover*. The *Ancon* was sold to the Marine Maritime Academy and became its training vessel *State of Maine*.

Beginning in 1961, Panama Line's terminus and administration offices were transferred from New York to New Orleans. From here it operated as a twelve-passenger freighter for a further twenty years, before retirement in 1981.

Pier 84, West 44th Street, American Export Lines

The painted words, 'American Export Lines' at the end of Pier 84 on West 44th Street were an icon in New York Harbor. Visitors to the port could not fail to see them and they will forever be in the memories of those who read these words either boarding or disembarking from liners docking in New York. The funnels of the ships were painted in a buff yellow with black tops and a white band edged with red.

American Export Lines began operations as the Export Steamship Corporation in 1919 with cargo services from New York to the Mediterranean. The word 'American' was first introduced to company marketing and advertising to emphasise the association with the US in the 1920s. A formal name change to American Export Lines was made in 1936. In 1964 the company merged with Isbrandtsen Co. to become American Export-Isbrandtsen Lines.

In 1931 the company placed in service four cargo passenger lines: *Excalibur*, *Excambion*, *Exeter* and *Exochorda*, known as 'the Four Aces'. The jewels in the crown of American Export Lines services using Pier 84 were the sister passenger liners SS *Constitution* and SS *Independence* and they were the first ocean liners built primarily for Mediterranean service. During the peak summer months these two superb ships operated a transatlantic express service between New York, Algeciras, Cannes, Genoa and Naples.

Each passenger class on both the *Constitution* and *Independence* was catered for, with a dining room, lounge and bar for each and outdoor swimming pools for first and cabin class. To the passenger they gave the impression of modern, well-maintained, sleek and speedy ships, yet without the exaggerated sense of luxury afforded on the Cunard Queen liners. In the early 1960s the livery on their hulls was changed to white to emphasise their cruising status. By 1968 both liners were affected by the transatlantic switch to jet aircraft travel and it was decided to lay both vessels up. Sadly, American Export Lines was reduced to a cargo firm and in 1978 was eventually bought out by Farrell Lines. The name American Export Lines was dropped and disappeared from Pier 84 with a coat of paint.

Pier 84, West 44th Street, Italian Line

Until 1963 American Export liners shared Pier 84, West 44th Street with the Italian Line, who was American Export Lines' great competitor. When Cunard moved from Pier 90 to 92 in the mid-1960s, the Italian Line moved its operations to the vacant Pier 90. Coincidentally, this also fitted in well with the introduction to service of the new Italian Line liners: *Michelangelo* and *Raffaello*. Italian Line ships had white funnels with a red top and a separate narrow green band.

The Italian Line or Italia Line, whose official name was Italia di Navigazione, provided a passenger service from New York to Italy and South America. In the late 1960s the company changed its focus to cruising and from 1981 it became a global freighter. Founded in 1932, through the merger of Navigazione Generale Italiana, Lloyd Sabaudo and Cosulich STN lines, the new company operated a sizeable fleet. The newly commissioned SS *Rex* captured the coveted Blue Riband in 1933, confirming that Italia Line was a leading shipping line on the Atlantic.

During the Second World War, the Italian Line lost many of its ships, including the *Rex* and the *Conte di Savoia*, and others were seized by the Allies and converted into troop and hospital ships. The company resumed commercial operations in 1947, under the new name Società di Navigazione Italia. In 1953 and 1954 two new ships were commissioned, *Andrea Doria* and *Cristoforo Colombo*. Tragedy was to strike, however, on the evening of Wednesday 25 July 1956, when the *Andrea Doria* collided with the Swedish ship *Stockholm* near Nantucket.

The *Andrea Doria*, commanded by Captain Piero Calamai, was carrying 1,134 passengers and 572 crew, and was heading towards New York. It was the last night of the voyage from Genoa and the liner was expected to dock at Pier 84 in New York the next morning. At the same time, the Swedish American Line MS *Stockholm*, commanded by Captain Harry Gunnar Nordenson, which had sailed from New York at about midday, was sailing at 18 knots east across from Ambrose Lightship towards Gothenburg, Sweden. On the *Andrea Doria* fog caused the captain to reduce speed to 21.8 knots, activate the ship's fog whistle and close the watertight doors, as per regulations in such conditions – the waters of the North Atlantic south of Nantucket Island are frequently the site of intermittent fog as the cold Labrador Current encounters the warm Gulf Stream. As the two ships approached each other at a combined speed of 40 knots, each was unable to see the other due to fog. Guided only by radar, the two ships misinterpreted each other's courses. The result was a disaster,

with the two ships colliding with each other almost at a 90-degree angle. *Stockholm*'s sharp ice-breaking prow pierced *Andrea Doria*'s starboard side approximately amidships, penetrating many occupied passenger cabins and gashing five fuel tanks which filled with 500 tons of seawater.

In the minutes after the collision, *Andrea Doria* started to list severely to starboard and the list increased to 18 degrees. Radio distress calls were sent out from both stricken vessels and soon a planned response was being co-ordinated by the US Coast Guard. On the *Stockholm*, the entire bow was crushed, including some cabins, resulting in the bow dipping dangerously. It was soon determined that despite having her first watertight compartment flooded, the *Stockholm* was in no imminent danger of sinking. On *Andrea Doria*, however, there were serious injuries and passengers were trapped in the mangled wreckage. Thirty minutes after the collision, the situation was deteriorating rapidly as the list increased and it became clear to those on the bridge that abandoning the ship was the only option.

The rescue effort was greatly assisted by the compassionate decision of Captain Baron Raoul de Beaudean to turn his eastbound French Line liner SS *Ile de France* around to assist the stricken *Andrea Doria*. The French liner had passed the Italian liner hours earlier and as the *Ile de France* returned cautiously back through the fog, the crew made ready to launch the lifeboats to receive survivors. Arriving at the scene in less than three hours, the fog lifted and the *Ile de France* was positioned in such a way that the *Andria Doria* was sheltered. All exterior lights on the *Ile de France* were turned on and it was said by survivors from the *Andrea Doria* that this had a great impact on morale.

By shuttling ten lifeboats back and forth to the *Andrea Doria*, passengers and crew from the Italian liner were soon in the warmth and safety of the French liner. Passengers on the *Ile de France* gave up their cabins to aid the wet, cold and tired survivors. Passengers and crew on the *Ile de France* then set about providing changes of clothing, hot drinks, food and comfort to the grateful survivors. Once the evacuation was complete, Captain Calamai of the *Andrea Doria* turned his attention to the salvage of his ship. However, the Italian liner began to roll, forcing the gallant captain to concede defeat and watch his once proud ship begin to sink at 9.45 a.m., eventually disappearing beneath the waves at 10.09 a.m. – almost exactly eleven hours after the collision.

The *Ile de France* returned to New York to a hero's welcome and was without doubt the saviour of the hour, but fifty-three people lost their lives in the disaster.

The Italian Line replaced the *Andrea Doria* with the larger and more technically advanced *Leonardo da Vinci*, which entered service in 1960. The Italian fleet was enlarged in 1965 by the addition of the *Michelangelo* and the *Raffaello*. They were both splendid luxury liners, equipped with six swimming pools, original Italian artworks, en-suite private cabins and stunning public rooms. The two new ships were designed for cruising as an alternative to operation on the Atlantic, but their use in this role proved problematic owing to the lack of modern facilities for comfort and entertainment purposes.

The Italian Line was now able to offer a sailing from New York every one to two weeks to Gibraltar, Naples, Cannes and Genoa. The two older ships were repainted with white hulls to fit with the stylish corporate image of the Italian Line. Sleek advertising campaigns in the US, showing off the Italian Line fleet, invited passengers to relax in style with a cruise from New York to the warmth of the Mediterranean.

Over the next few years the transatlantic service from New York began to incur huge financial losses and in 1976 the service ceased. The *Leonardo de Vinci* was withdrawn from service, joining the *Michelangelo* and *Raffaello* which had suffered the same fate the previous year. By 1980 the Italian Line had turned away from all cruising and passenger services operating from New York to concentrate on container and freight operation.

Above: The Italian Line *Giulio Cesare* is seen resting at Pier 84, West 44th Street, in August 1958. *Britton Collection*

Right: The stricken and doomed Italian Liner *Andrea Doria* is taking on water and listing prior to her sinking, following collision with the *Stockholm* in July 1956. *Press Association*

Above: Cunard Atlantic sailings, 1966.

The French Line SS *Ile de France* is seen rescuing passengers and crew from the doomed Italian Line *Andrea Doria*, which is seen severely listing prior to sinking in July 1956. *US Coast Guard*

The whistles blow and echo around Manhattan at the very moment of sailing from Pier 84, West 44th Street, of the Italian Line *Leonardo da Vinci* on 21 August 1965. Black exhaust smoke pours out of the funnel, indicating that the captain has ordered the ship to sail slowly out into the Hudson River assisted by a Moran tugboat. Note the crowds of passengers watching the proceedings from the forward observation deck located at the base of the forward mast above the bridge. *Britton Collection*

Here the damaged *Stockholm* is under repair following her fateful collision with the Italian Line *Andrea Doria* in July 1956. *Associated Press*

Rust stains on the hull from the anchor of the Italian Line *Leonardo da Vinci* catch the eye in this evocative picture. The name *Leonardo da Vinci* is almost masked by thick mooring ropes. *Britton Collection*

Right: An Italian Line 'Caribbean cruise' leaflet.

Below: An Italian Line first-class ticket.

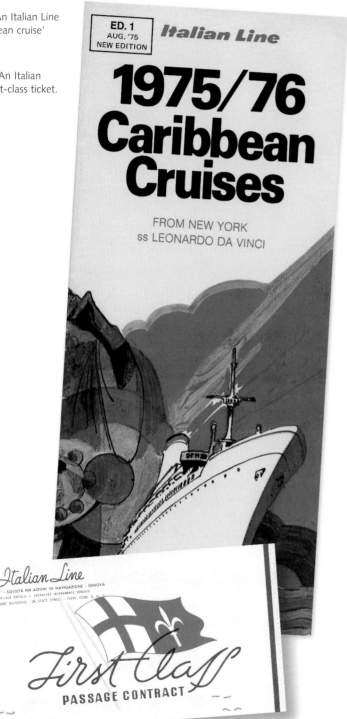

Right: Italian Line luggage label.

Pier 86, West 46th Street, United States Lines

Pier 86, West 46th Street in the 1950s and 1960s was the favourite place to be in New York for many shipping and liner enthusiasts. Here it was possible to observe the arrivals and sailings of the most technologically advanced passenger liners in the world, operated by the United States Lines. United States Lines ships had dark red funnels with a white band and blue top. On sailing days there was always a great buzz of boarding passengers checking in, the crew making ready, porters heaving enormous trunks, a queue of yellow taxi cabs and excited visitors and spectators. The spectacle was often added to by the sound of a band serenading passengers and visitors. Forget the Broadway theatres with their 'big star-studied shows'; Pier 86 was the place to have a ticket for a ringside seat.

United States Lines was formed to operate transatlantic cargo services in 1921 using three ships from the United States Mail Steamship Company. Two of these ships were First World War reparations. Additional ships were acquired in 1922 and renamed after former United States Presidents. In 1923 the 52,000-ton *Vaterland* was added to the fleet and renamed *Leviathan*. The line was sold in 1929 to P.W. Chapman Co. and reorganised as United States Lines Inc. of Delaware. Two years later, after the Stock Market crash, the ships were sold to United States Lines Company of Nevada.

In 1932 and 1933, the fleet was added to with the *Manhattan* and *Washington*. In 1940 the *America* joined the growing United States Lines fleet. During the Second World War the ships were converted for war service as troopships. The *Manhattan* was renamed USS *Wakefield*, the *Washington* became the USS *Mount Vernon* and the newest flagship liner, the *America*, became the USS *West Point*.

The post-war period saw the *America* having to cope with the transatlantic service single-handed until 1952 when, with government subsidy, a new superliner was constructed with the aim of capturing the transatlantic speed record. The new $78 million liner, designed by the renowned American naval architect William Francis Gibbs, lived up to her billing and swept all before her, easily capturing the prestigious Blue Riband, both east and west bound, for the fastest Atlantic passenger-ship crossing. New York savoured the victory of the victorious SS *United States* when she returned to Pier 86 in July 1952.

The dawn of the jet age saw passenger numbers at Pier 86 begin to dwindle. By 1964 the competition from the air caused the United States Lines to sell the *America* to Chandris Line and five years later the *United States* was mothballed with the termination of passenger services to Le Havre, Southampton and Bremerhaven. The United States Lines continued to offer container ship services until being bought out by Malcolm McLean in 1987.

Above: An American classic car is parked in front of the United States Lines SS *America* at Pier 85. Today they would both be highly prized antiques. *Britton Collection*

Above right: The sharp-pointed stem of the SS *United States* receives some touching up from painters at Pier 86. This was a dangerous job, balancing on precarious planks and rope ladders, and it wasn't for those who were afraid of heights. *Britton Collection*

Right: A superb aerial view of the Chandris Lines SS *Australis*, the former United States Lines SS *America*, pictured sailing into New York. *World Ship Society*

Above: SS *United States* cabin class luggage labels.

Above: An SS *United States* first-class luggage label.

Left: SS *United States* sailing schedule 1958.

SS *United States* tourist-class luggage labels.

Pier 86, West 46th Street, Incres Line

From 1950 less glamorous visitors to Pier 86, West 46th Street, were the ships belonging to the Incress Line, which took low-budget tourist class and immigrants across the Atlantic. Initially this budget shipping used the former 15,043-ton P&O ship *Mongolia*, briefly renamed *Europa* and then *Nassau*. In early 1960, the former Union-Castle Line *Dunnottar Castle* joined the Incres fleet, working from Pier 86 cruising to the Caribbean. The Incres Line ships had yellow funnels with a narrow blue top. Clipper Line of Sweden acquired Incres Line in 1964, but ceased operating in 1975.

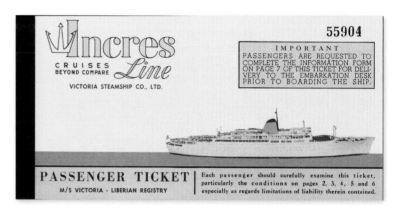

An Incres Line ticket.

SS *United States* 'wanted on voyage' labels.

Pier 88, West 48th Street, French Line

The Compagnie Generale Transatlantique (CGT), with its base at Pier 88 West 48th Street, was better known in New York as Transat or the French Line. The French Line ships had dark red-coloured funnels with a black top. It had the reputation for being the owner of the most glamorous and beautiful-looking liners to sail from New York. Passengers on board enjoyed a lifestyle of luxury with impeccable cuisine, luxurious décor and unsurpassed service.

Established in 1861, the company's first vessel, SS *Washington*, had her maiden voyage on 15 June 1864. However, it was not until after the First World War that the French Line became a major operator on the Atlantic from New York. In 1927, the people of New York welcomed French Line's luxury liner the *Ile de France*, which was the first liner to be styled in art deco. In 1935 the French overnment subsidised the company to build arguably the most beautiful liner to ever cross the Atlantic and enter New York, the *Normandie*. When launched she was the largest liner in the world and was soon to become the fastest, seizing the Blue Riband from the Italian liner *Rex* on her first voyage, which she completed at an average speed of 30 knots. Visitors to the ship after arriving in New York were astounded by the art deco interior and sweeping streamlined hull design. She instantly became a favourite at Pier 88 in New York, but sadly this was the scene of her destruction when she caught fire here in 1942.

After the Second World War, French Line acquired the former German liner *Europa* as part of war reparations. She was given a $16 million refit and emerged in August 1950 as *Liberté*. The most obvious change in her appearance was the repainting of her funnels from North German Lloyd yellow livery to the characteristic CGT red funnels with black tops. In 1954 her funnels were heightened and small fins added, which gave her an even more distinctive appearance. Later the funnels were capped, but with a service speed of 24 knots she was never a contender for the Blue Riband.

French Line passenger traffic from Pier 88 at New York grew in the post-war period until the advent of the transatlantic jet aircraft. Despite the addition to the French Line fleet of the 66,000-ton *France* in 1961, which was the longest liner in the world, passenger numbers continued to drift away and switch to air travel. French government subsidies ended in 1974 and the *France* was laid up until 1979 when she was sold to the Norwegian Caribbean Line (NCL) for conversion to cruising and renamed *Norway*.

The *France* was the last of the great French Line Atlantic liners to operate from New York designed for operating across the Atlantic. She had a greater speed than the Cunard Queens and could easily maintain a five-day crossing schedule with a fortnightly round trip from New York to Le Havre and Southampton. Her demise signalled the end of an era.

Left: French Line SS *Ile de France* cabin-class plan.

Below left and right: Lifeboats are being lowered from the port side of the French Line *Normandie* at Pier 88 as part of the routine lifeboat drill practice for the crew in July 1938. *Britton Collection*

New York welcomes the French Line SS *Liberté* on her maiden voyage on 23 August 1950. *Associated Press*

Left: *Deux panaches de fumée noire s'échappent de la cheminée.* (Two plumes of black smoke escape from the funnel.) *Dave Witmer/Britton Collection*

Below left: *Le départ du premier voyage du paquebot* le France *sur le Hudson glacé, février 1962.* (The departure on its maiden voyage of the SS *France* down the ice-covered Hudson River, February 1962.) *Britton Collection*

Below right: The French Line *Liberté* reappeared after her winter overhaul of 1953–54 fitted with enormous domed top funnels. They made the 51,839-ton liner look even bigger. When she entered Pier 88, West 44th Street, New York, the unsuspecting local shipping enthusiasts stood and gasped. *Britton Collection*

Far left: A French Line leaflet.

Left: French Line luggage label to Le Havre.

Pier 88, West 48th Street, Greek Line

Frequent visitors to Pier 88 were ships from the Greek Line, which was formally known as the General Steam Navigation Company of Greece. The Greek Line was owned by the Ormos Shipping Company and operated services from New York to Europe, mostly using a fleet of second-hand ships between 1939 and 1975. The company began to diversify into leisure cruising with the onset of the jet age. Greek Line's only new-build ship was the *Olympia*, which was laid up in 1974. On their funnels, the Greek Line ships had a trident device painted on a broad blue band between a black top and yellow base.

Pier 88, West 48th Street, North German Lloyd

North German Lloyd (NDL) ships were a familiar sight with their plain yellow funnels at Pier 88 and in the 1950s and '60s. They were very popular vessels on the New York waterfront scene. Their sailings from Pier 88 were just after midnight, or, to be precise, one minute after midnight. This NDL sailing was always a colourful and festive occasion for passengers. A traditional Bavarian oompah band, reminiscent of a German Bier Keller, would strike up a lively foot-stomping, thigh-slapping tune as the ship slowly reversed out into the Hudson River, while passengers sipped cool, refreshing Oettinger or Krombacher German beers.

The origins of the company date back to 20 February 1857, when it was founded by Hermann Henrich Meier and Eduard Crusemann in the northern German city of Bremen. It was to become one of the most important shipping companies to operate services in New York in the

A close-up of a lifeboat of the TS *Bremen* at Pier 88, West 48th Street, reveals that it could carry 146 persons. *Britton Collection*

Dressed overall, the North German Lloyd TS *Bremen* looks like a beautiful lady at Pier 88, West 48th Street, in August 1969. *Britton Collection*

The first routine on board the SS *Niew Amsterdam* after sailing from Pier 88, West 48th Street, in August 1969 is the lifeboat drill. *Britton Collection*

Looking resplendent in the sunlight at Pier 88 is the North German Lloyd *Europa*, with her black hull, white superstructure and mustard-coloured funnels. She was originally built as the *Kungsholm* in 1953, but was sold to North German Lloyd in 1965. *Britton Collection*

nineteenth and twentieth centuries. North German Lloyd really came to the fore in New York between the wars when, in 1929 and 1930, the company placed into service the 51,656-ton *Bremen* and the 49,746-ton *Europa*. Both ships made their mark on the Atlantic by taking the Blue Riband for the fastest Atlantic crossings.

The Second World War had a devastating effect on NDL, as its entire fleet was either lost or awarded to the Allies as reparations. The prize asset, the *Europa*, was claimed by the French and became the *Liberté*. It was not until 1951, when the Allied restrictions on German shipping were lifted, that NDL could plan for the future and build a new fleet. At first the company purchased old freighters to gain a foothold in shipping, but passenger services across the Atlantic to New York did not resume until 1955. The former 1924-built Swedish ship MS *Gripsholm* was refitted and renamed *Berlin*. In 1959 NDL added the former French Line 32,336-ton *Pasteur* to the fleet and renamed her *Bremen*. This was followed, in 1965, by the former Swedish American Line's 21,514-ton *Kungsholm*, which was renamed *Europa*. The NDL liners made an impressive sight sailing up the Hudson into New York, but the downturn in passenger receipts on the Atlantic service forced NDL to transfer its fleet to cruising. By 1968 NDL began moving away from passenger services to concentrate and develop its container operation from New York. On 1 September 1970, North German Lloyd merged with Hamburg America Line to form Hapag-Lloyd. Passenger services from New York were suspended soon after.

Piers 90 and 92, West 50th and 52nd Street, Cunard Line

The name Cunard was an iconic name on the Atlantic and dominated passenger services to Europe from New York during the twentieth century. The red funnels with their black tops and thin black rings of the Cunard White Star Line were familiar to New Yorkers passing Piers 90 and 92. The exception being the funnel of the MV *Britannic*, the last of the old White Star Line, which had buff-coloured funnels with black tops.

It was in 1839 that Samuel Cunard, a Nova Scotian, was awarded the first transatlantic steamship mail contract and for the next thirty years the Cunard Line dominated the North Atlantic. By 1902, to regain the Blue Riband in the face of stiff competition, the British Government subsidised the construction of two new liners, *Mauretania* and *Lusitania*. In the late 1920s fresh challenges to Cunard came from the French, Germans and Italians. Cunard responded by constructing RMS *Queen Mary*, but was forced to suspend operation because of the Great Depression. In 1934 the British Government offered Cunard financial assistance to complete the *Queen Mary*, which entered service in 1936, providing that Cunard merged with the ailing White Star Line. The result was the formation of Cunard White Star.

Cunard had great plans to operate the Atlantic service from New York with two Queen superliners. The construction of the three-funnel *Queen Mary* was followed by a larger two-funnel sister, *Queen Elizabeth*. However, the completion of the *Queen Elizabeth* at John Brown & Co. on the Clyde was interrupted by the Second World War and the great dream for a two-Queen ship service across the Atlantic had to be postponed until after the war. Instead, the two Queens were to enter war service, at first in the Pacific and later across the Atlantic. British Prime Minister Winston Churchill was to write in his memoirs that the Cunard Queen ships shortened the Second World War by at least a year.

After the war, when Cunard purchased White Star's remaining shareholding in 1947, the name reverted to Cunard Line. Having secured control, Cunard commissioned five freighters and two cargo liners in 1947. Two years later a new luxury permanent cruise liner RMS *Caronia* entered service in the Cunard fleet. The last four-funnel transatlantic

'Have you anything to declare?' A scene rarely, if ever, recorded at the Cunard Pier 90, West 50th Street, was the customs hall. This picture dates from December 1964. *Britton Collection*

liner, RMS *Aquitania*, was sent to the scrap yard in 1950 and Cunard restructured for a modern post-war future with the marketing slogan, 'Getting there is half the fun'. The last remnant of the White Star Line, MS *Britannic*, remained in service, calling at New York until 1960.

During the 1960s, Cunard receipts for services across the Atlantic began to diminish. Radical changes were called for to tackle the increasing decline.

First the *Queen Mary* was sold off into retirement to the city of Long Beach in 1967, to be followed by the *Queen Elizabeth* in the following year. The year-round Cunard service from New York to Europe therefore came to an end in 1968. With the introduction of the *Queen Elizabeth 2* (*QE2*), Cunard concentrated on cruising and summer transatlantic voyages only.

Above left: Showing signs of her age and looking the worse for wear and a rough Atlantic crossing, the Cunard RMS *Queen Mary* is propelled out into the Hudson by two Moran tugs. *Britton Collection*

Above right: New York Central Railroad steam tug No. 16 is seen paying her last respects to the Cunard RMS *Queen Mary*, which is berthed at Pier 90 on 22 September 1967. *Britton Collection*

Left: The tugboat *Kerry Moran* is taking up position at Cunard Pier 90, West 50th Street, to propel the RMS *Caronia* on 3 July 1964. *Britton Collection*

Above: Cunard 'Not Wanted' label.

Left: The Cunard *Queen Elizabeth 2* (*QE2*) completes her maiden voyage arrival at New York escorted by an admiring flotilla of Moran tugs and pleasure craft. *World Ship Society*

CUNARD
LINE

PLEASE COMPLETE IN BLOCK LETTERS

M

SHIP

CLASS   DATE OF
                         SAILING

FROM   TO

ADDRESS IN
U.S.A OR
CANADA

NOT WANTED
ON THE VOYAGE

Pier 95, West 55th Street, Furness-Bermuda Line

The regular sight of Furness Bermuda Line ships, with their dark red with black top funnels with a black base and black band, sailing each week from Pier 95 in New York was something one could almost set the time by. These popular ships were known to many as the 'honeymoon cruises' for newlyweds setting out on the first part of their lives together. To others the voyages were known as the 'millionaire cruises'. Indeed, it is said that wealthy Americans would regularly tip crew members with $50 and $100 bill notes. One senior middle-aged millionaire businessman, on receiving a positive reply to an offer of marriage from a glamorous young American beauty, even tipped a steward $1,000 with free drinks and cigars all round in celebration!

The Furness Bermuda Line was founded in 1919, after it had won a contract to build a postal service between New York and Bermuda. Throughout the roaring 1920s the service expanded with the development of passenger services. The service reached its zenith just before the Second World War, when two new luxury liners were commissioned to be built by Vickers Armstrong in its Tyne shipbuilding yards in England. These two beautifully proportioned three-funnel sister ships were called *Monarch of Bermuda* and *Queen of Bermuda* and sailed on the cruise run from New York to Bermuda, which took only forty hours in each direction. Without doubt, they were the elite ships of their day and had private facilities in their cabins, resulting in them having a reputation for unsurpassed luxury.

When war was declared in 1939, both of these luxury liners were drafted by the British Government into wartime service. The *Queen of Bermuda* was at first converted to an armed merchant cruiser before being refitted to join the *Monarch of Bermuda* as a troop transport ship. Sadly after the war the *Monarch of Bermuda* suffered serve fire damage. She was salvaged and after repair was refitted as an emigrant ship. Fortunately the *Queen of Bermuda* returned to service in 1947 to continue her long and distinguished service working from New York to Bermuda. In May 1951 the fleet was strengthened with the introduction of the 13,500-ton *Ocean Monarch*.

Between October 1961 and March 1962 the *Queen of Bermuda* was transformed and modernised while being refitted. She emerged as a one-funnel – all air-conditioned ship. The bow was also lengthened by 8ft. On her return to Pier 95, the ship was given a fireboat salute, the traditional New York reception for new ships. The new lease of life was not to last long however, as in 1966 the US Coast Guard introduced new safety standards and legislation for all vessels using ports in the United States. With an estimated cost of millions of dollars to upgrade the ship to the new demanding standards, it was decided to withdraw the veteran *Queen of Bermuda* and she made her final sailing into New York on Saturday 19 November 1966, before Captain M.E. Musson sailed her on her last, lonely voyage across the Atlantic for scrapping at Faslane on the River Clyde in Scotland.

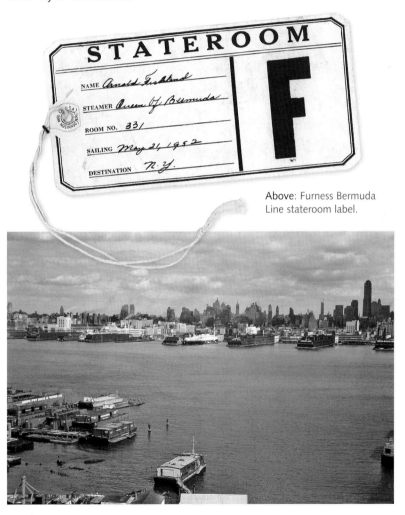

Above: Furness Bermuda Line stateroom label.

A view from the other side of the Hudson River looking towards the Atlantic Terminal Luxury Liner Row piers. Pier 93 is occupied by the Cunard RMS *Britannic* and the three-funnel Furness Bermuda Line *Queen of Bermuda* is seen at Pier 95. *Britton Collection*

Pier 95, West 55th Street, Canadian Pacific

The white-hulled Canadian Pacific liners, with their yellow and red and white chequered panels, were an impressive sight as they made their way up the Hudson River to dock at Pier 95, West 55th Street.

Canadian Pacific began with trans-Pacific services in 1887 and it was not until 1903 that the company expanded operations to run across the Atlantic from Halifax and Nova Scotia to Britain. After the First World War, the Canadian Pacific purchased eleven new steamships to replace its fleet losses. The result was the construction of the famed Empress Class of ships, which included such illustrious liners as the RMS *Empress of Australia*, RMS *Empress of Britain*, SS *Duchess of Bedford* (later renamed the *Empress of France*) and the SS *Duchess of Richmond* (later renamed RMS *Empress of Canada*). Canadian Pacific continued to carry passengers, freight and mail across the Atlantic, but after the Second World War it introduced winter cruising from New York to the Caribbean.

Between 1956 and 1961, Canadian Pacific acquired three more steam passenger ships: RMS *Empress of England*, RMS *Empress of Canada* and the new RMS *Empress of Britain*. By the mid-1960s competition from the airlines forced Canadian Pacific to cease its passenger ship operations and concentrate on the new and growing container market.

Pier 97, West 57th Street, Swedish American Line and Home Lines

Pier 97, West 57th Street was the home of the Swedish American Line, otherwise known as the 'White Viking Fleet'. This affectionate nickname related to its all-white livery hull and superstructure appearance. The popular Swedish American Line ships had yellow funnels with three yellow crowns set on a blue disc.

The company was founded in December 1914 to offer ocean liner services from Sweden to North America, under the name *Rederiaktiebolaget Sverige-Nordamerika*, which when translated is Shipping Corporation Sweden-North America. The Swedes had the foresight to build liners with the provision for off-peak cruising and also be the first shipping company to construct a diesel-engined transatlantic liner.

Initially the Swedish American Line concentrated on the immigrant traffic to North America. The service continued during the First World War until 1917, when unrestricted submarine warfare caused the suspension of service. In June 1918 the passenger service from Gothenburg resumed

and flourished in the inter-war years. The *Gripsholm* was launched on 26 November 1924 and made her maiden voyage to New York on 21 November 1925. Encouraged by the success of the *Gripsholm*, the Swedish American Line decided to expand and enter the cruise market in 1927 and added to the fleet with the construction of the larger MS *Kungsholm* in March 1928. The new *Kungsholm* worked into New York with capacity for 1,344, but this was reduced to 600 when cruising. Internally she was a most impressive ship with her art deco style.

During the Second World War the *Kungsholm* stopped her transatlantic services in October 1939, but continued cruising from New York to the Caribbean until 1941. Meanwhile, other members of the fleet, the *Gripsholm* and *Drottingholm*, were laid up in New York. Both ships were taken into war service by the US Government when the USA entered the war in 1941. The *Gripsholm* sailed under the auspices of the International Red Cross, with a Swedish captain and Swedish crew, as an exchange and repatriation vessel carrying German and Japanese nationals to exchange points. She would then return with US and Canadian citizens to New York.

After the war, on 26 March 1946, the Swedish American Line re-commenced transatlantic services between Gothenburg and New York. On 9 September 1946, the newly built MS *Stockholm* strengthened operational services.

During 1946 the Swedish American Line founded Home Lines, which also operated from Pier 97 in New York. By 1948 Home Lines had acquired three second-hand ships: the *Bergensfjord* from Norwegian American Line, renamed *Argentina*, and the Swedish American liners *Drottningholm* and *Kungsholm*, renamed *Brasil* and *Italia* respectively.

On 30 September 1953 the Swedish American Line had a new ship delivered, MS *Kungsholm*, which was the third ship to bear this name. Another new vessel entered into the line's service in April 1956, the MS *Gripsholm*, which was the second ship to bear this name in the fleet. A few months later tragedy struck when the Swedish American Line's *Stockholm* collided with the SS *Andrea Doria*, which resulted in the loss of five members of crew in addition to the considerable loss of life on the *Andrea Doria*. The *Stockholm* was able to return to New York where she was repaired at the Bethlehem Steel shipyards, re-entering service on 5 November 1956.

Anticipating growth in transatlantic passenger services and cruising from New York, the Swedish American Line ordered another new ship in August 1963. The ship was built at John Brown & Co., Scotland, and named MS *Kungsholm* (the fourth ship to bear the name). The old *Kungsholm* was sold

Above: A brace of cruise ships sail from New York: the 18,017-ton Chandris Line SS *Britanis* sailing to Bermuda with 1,200 passengers and the Home Lines 39,241-ton SS *Oceanic* sailing to Nassau on a seven-day cruise, ably assisted by Moran tugboats. *Jim Gavin*

Below: Resting at Pier 97, West 57th Street, is the popular 641ft Home Lines SS *Homeric*, which regularly sailed from New York to Nassau, Bahamas. She first visited New York in January 1955. This 18,563-ton liner was originally named SS *Mariposa* and was originally designed for service in the Pacific Ocean for Matson Lines. She sailed on her maiden voyage on 16 January 1932. *Britton Collection*

Above: The maiden voyage arrival of the Swedish American Line *Kungsholm* at New York, 3 December 1953. *Associated Press*

to NDL on 5 October 1965 and continued to run into New York renamed MS *Europa*. By April 1966, when the new *Kungsholm* entered service, passenger numbers between Gothenburg to New York had substantially reduced and after just nine crossings, the new ship was transferred to world cruises. Within a decade, in August 1975, the *Gripsholm* and the *Kungsholm* were taken out of service and laid up, despite protests from the company's US offices.

ACROSS THE RIVER HUDSON: JERSEY CITY

Pier 9, American President Lines

American President Lines was formed in 1938, when the US Government took over the management of the Dollar Steamship Company, which was in financial difficulty. By 1940 sixteen new ships were commissioned, each named after a former president of the USA. When the US entered the war, the fleet of ships were drafted in to assist with the war effort.

After the Second World War, American President Lines started a round-the-world service from New York and added to the fleet with the *President Cleveland* and *President Wilson*. A new marketing strategy was implemented with the advertising slogan, 'Your American hotel abroad'. This campaign was successful and the company expanded between 1952 and 1954 by ordering eleven more ships.

An imaginative change in direction came in 1958, when American President Lines began to explore the possibility of containerisation. In 1961 containerisation was introduced with the launching of two new ships capable of container transport, *President Tyler* and *President Lincoln*. By the end of the decade containerisation accounted for an increasing proportion of the company's business and by 1973 the last liner in operation, *President Wilson*, completed her final round-the-world voyage and was sold off.

Today American President Lines, or NPL as it is known, is a world leader in container shipping and continues to operate from New York.

HOBOKEN

Pier B, 5th and 6th Street Piers, Holland America Line

The piers at 5th and 6th Street in Hoboken were the western hub of the Holland America Line's transatlantic services from the late nineteenth century until the opening of Pier 40 in 1963. The Dutch liners were noted in New York for their reliability and pristine appearance with their weekly three-ship operation. During the peak season, a Holland America Line ship would sail from Hoboken every Friday for Southampton, Le Havre and Rotterdam. The Holland America Line ships had their funnels painted yellow with a white band set between two green bands.

The flagship and most beautiful ship of the Holland America Line fleet regularly seen in New York was the 758ft-long *Nieuw Amsterdam*, with accommodation for 574 first and 583 tourist passengers. She was built before the Second World War and the Dutch proclaimed her as, 'the ship of tomorrow'. Internally she was an art deco maritime icon.

An icy Hudson River greets the Holland America Line SS *Nieuw Amsterdam* at the 5th Street Pier, Hoboken, in January 1963. *Britton Collection*

Taken from the portside deck of the outbound Holland America Line's SS *Statendam*, we see the inbound North German Lloyd SS *Berlin* heading up the Hudson. *Britton Collection*

Hundreds of faces gaze up at the decks of the departing SS *Ile de France* at the end of the French Line Pier 88, West 48th Street – some sad, some excited and many just curious and overcome by the sheer size of the enormous French liner. *Britton Collection*

The maiden-voyage arrival of the SS *France* on 8 February 1962 at the French Line Pier 88, West 48th Street, was a joyful and exciting occasion. A flight of US Coast Guard helicopters flew over the 66,343-ton liner, which at 1,035ft was the longest passenger liner in the world at the time. *Britton Collection*

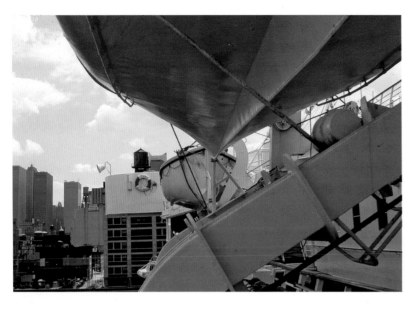

Looking forwards from the lifeboat deck on the SS *France*, the giant skyscrapers of Manhattan confirm that the French Line flagship is berthed at Pier 88, West 48th Street. *Britton Collection*

A close-up view taken on board the *Liberté*, showing the letters of the name, which were illuminated by electric light bulbs after darkness. *Britton Collection*

Le départ du premier voyage du paquebot le France *sur le Hudson glacé, février 1962.* (The departure on her maiden voyage of the SS *France* down the ice-covered Hudson River, February 1962.) *Britton Collection*

Above: The view from the bridge of the TS *Bremen* at Pier 88 in New York. *Britton Collection*

Left: Looking back from a tugboat we are able to appreciate a little of the enormity of the 32,336-ton TS *Bremen*. Originally this magnificent ship was the French Line *Pasteur*, built in 1938. In September 1957 she was sold for DM30 million to the North German Lloyd Line. After refit, one very noticeable change in her visual appearance was a new drop-shaped funnel, which made the ship more aesthetically appealing in proportion. To enhance comfort, two stabilisers were fitted and on 9 July 1959 the TS *Bremen* was placed on the Bremerhaven–Southampton–Cherbourg–New York service. In 1971, when North German Lloyd merged with the Hamburg America Line, she transferred her operations to cruising and made her final Bremerhaven to New York voyage in September 1971. A month later the *Bremen* was sold to the Greek Chandris Cruises shipping line. *Britton Collection*

The bridge of the TS *Bremen* at Pier 88, West 48th Street, New York. The smell of polish and Brasso filled the nostrils and the instruments sparkled. *Britton Collection*

A view down the port-side Promenade deck of the TS *Bremen* at Pier 88, West 48th Street. *Britton Collection*

Looking forward across Manhattan on the starboard-side lifeboat deck of the TS *Bremen* at Pier 88, West 48th Street. *Britton Collection*

The 'oompah band' strikes up a rousing Bavarian foot-stomping tune as the TS *Bremen* sails from Pier 88, West 48th Street. *Britton Collection*

The North German Lloyd *Berlin* was the first post-war West German fleet member. She was originally built as the Swedish *Gripsholm* in 1925 and is pictured here at Pier 97, West 57th Street. *Britton Collection*

Now just a memory, the Cunard Line Pier 92, West 52nd Street, was built in 1935 for the RMS *Queen Mary*. *Britton Collection*

The entrance of a Queen: the Cunard RMS *Queen Elizabeth* enters Pier 90 at West 50th Street in May 1966, assisted by four Moran tugs at the starboard bow and a further tug at the stern. *Marc Piche*

It was always a great pleasure to see the 35,738-ton Cunard RMS *Mauretania* sail. Here she is seen departing from Pier 90 in April 1954, assisted by two Moran tugs, taking cooks to Europe. *Britton Collection*

Above: Give us a wave! Crowds of well-wishers wave from the public gallery at Cunard Pier 9o, West 52nd Street. *Britton Collection*

The Canadian Pacific *Empress of Canada* prepares to make a smoky departure from Pier 95, West 55th Street, in December 1969. When the St Lawrence River in Canada was ice-bound during the winter months, some of the Canadian Pacific liners transferred their operational services south to New York, using Piers 95 and 97. *Britton Collection*

Left: The maiden voyage arrival of a liner at New York was always a very special occasion. Here we see North German LLoyd MS *Europa* at Pier 87 in January 1966 in her black hull, white superstructure and mustard-coloured funnels. To the left in Pier 86 is the SS *United States*, which is being refuelled and cleared of rubbish to and from the adjacent barges. *Britton Collection*

A gorgeous sunset shot of the 580ft-long Furness Bermuda Line *Queen of Bermuda* docking at Pier 95 West 55th Street. This beautiful three-funnelled liner had three very distinctive steam whistles that would echo across Manhattan on Saturdays at 3 p.m. when she sailed to Bermuda. *Britton Collection*

The popular 641ft Home Lines SS *Homeric* regularly sailed from New York to Nassau, Bahamas. She first visited New York in January 1955. This 18,563-ton liner was originally named SS *Mariposa* and was designed for service in the Pacific Ocean for Matson Lines, sailing on her maiden voyage on 16 January 1932. In this close up view, she is surrounded by ice from the Hudson River. *Britton Collection*

Regal splendour. The glowing lights on board the French Line *Liberté* were a magnificent piece of self-advertising in this view taken at the French Line Pier 88, West 48th Street in 1954. *Earl Osborn/Britton Collection*

Left: During the hours of darkness, Luxury Liner Row in New York took on a new, magical dimension. The famous piers were proudly illuminated with the names of the shipping line companies, the floodlit liners sparkled with silvery lights from every porthole and the gigantic funnels shone out across Manhattan like glowing beacons. In this superb shot we can see *Victoria*, Cunard RMS *Queen Elizabeth* and *Kungsholm* on the 22 March 1968. *Britton Collection*

Below left: The famous funnels of the Cunard RMS *Queen Elizabeth*, lit by the line's own floodlights, shine out like a flaming red torch across the Manhattan skyline. The *Queen Elizabeth* had two funnels. The forward funnel was over 70ft in height from the sun deck and the after funnel was slightly less. *Ernest Arroyo/David Boone Collection*

Below: At night-time a walk or drive along the waterfront of Manhattan was a very different experience from that by day, and often cars would pause for drivers and passengers to gaze at an illuminated liner. Here the Italian liner *Cristoforo Columbus* slumbers at Pier 84, West 44th Street, in May 1965. *Britton Collection*

Like a glittering golden angel in the darkness, the *Europa* glows radiating warmth from her funnels, reflected in the still waters on 22 March 1968. *Britton Collection*

An occasional visitor to New York was the P&O Line *Himalaya*, seen here sparkling in the darkness. *Britton Collection*

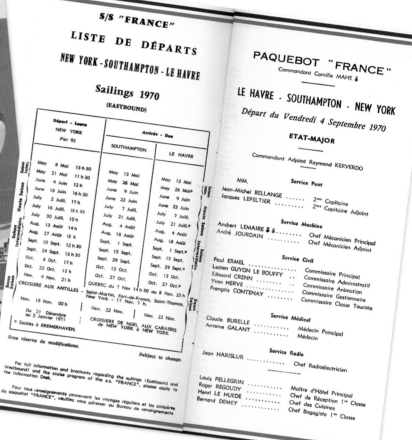

Above left: Advertisement for Cunard Atlantic sailings in 1964.

Above right: A French Line SS *France* sailing schedule.

Left: A Cunard Stateroom baggage label.

Above: A Furness Bermuda Line brochure.

Above: A Grace Line ticket holder.

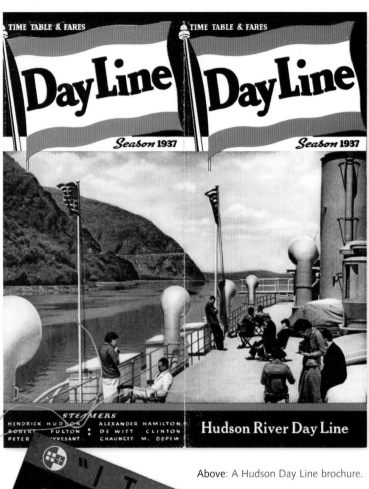

Above: A Hudson Day Line brochure.

Right: Furness Bermuda Line luggage label.

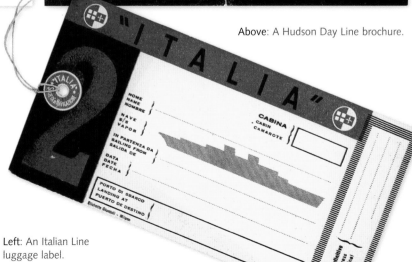

Left: An Italian Line luggage label.

83

Right: The sailing of SS *United States* under the Verrazano Narrows Bridge on its opening day is commemorated.

Below: An SS *United States* passenger booklet.

SS *United States* baggage stickers for first class, cabin class and tourist class.

Left: New York Central Railroad steam tugboat No. 18, which was built in 1913, is pictured in action on 21 January 1964, towing snow-covered railroad boxcars on a car float. *Britton Collection*

Below left: The tugboat *Kerry Moran* takes up position at Cunard Pier 90, West 50th Street, to propel the RMS Caronia, on 3 July 1964. *Britton Collection*

Below right: TA veteran steam tug is seen tied up at South Street Pier 17. *Britton Collection*

A New York fireboat provides a spectacular display on 27 April 1963. *Britton Collection*

Photographer Jim Gavin has captured an impressive action shot through his lens of the modern diesel tugboat *James Turecamo* on 4 June 1982. *Jim Gavin*

Photographer Jim Gavin was in position bright and early to record this superb picture of a fireboat salute to the SS *Atlantic* heading out on her maiden voyage on 7 September 1983. *Jim Gavin*

Perhaps often overlooked subjects to photograph in New York were the support vessels. Here is one such vessel, the W.M. Rogers Corporation crane barge number 15 on 13 April 1968. *Britton Collection*

A fine line-up of New York tugboats at New Jersey in November 1960. From left toright: B&O Railroad tugs *Walter L. Price* and *Howard E. Simpson*, and Central Railroad of New Jersey tugboat *Communipaw. Britton Collection*

A view of the New York Central Railroad ferry terminal in July 1958.

A view of the New York Central Railroad ferry terminal taken in July 1958. *Britton Collection*

Above: A close-up view of one of the characteristic funnels of Lackawanna steam ferries, *Scranton. Britton Collection*

Above right: Withdrawn from service and no longer wanted, the ferry *Elmira* awaits her fate in October 1975. How many thousands of commuters must have crossed the Hudson on this delightful antique? *Britton Collection*

Right: Here is a view of a then modern diesel City of New York Marine & Aviation ferry crossing the Hudson in September 1965. *Britton Collection*

The Holland America Line SS *Rotterdam* carves a path through the icy Hudson River in January at the end of her voyage from Europe to 5th Street Pier at Hoboken.

Todds Shipyards always seemed to act like a magnet to enthusiastic young shipping buffs, especially when it was snowy. Peeping through the gates in March 1964 it was possible to catch a glimpse of the American Export SS *Independence* elevated out of the water in a floating dry dock. What a wonderful sight. *Britton Collection*

For sale, United States Lines SS *America*! She has made her final voyage on the New York-Le Havre-Bremerhaven-Southampton-Cobh service for the United States Line. This 1963 picture shows the once pride of the United States Line at Todds shipyard for an assessment check following withdrawal, pending sale to the Chandris Line and exchange of contracts. *Britton Collection*

An evocative view of of the SS *Caprella* tanker in June 1966 and her refit in dry dock at Todds shipyard. *Britton Collection*

American classic cars abound in front of the smoky freighter SS *Hong Kong* of the Orient Overseas Line. This typical scene from the 1960s was just as much a part of New York Harbor as the more prestigious ocean liners at the Atlantic Terminal piers. *Britton Collection*

The Brooklyn Pier 4 of the Arthur Tickle Engineering Works with the stunning backdrop of Lower Manhattan made this a memorable location for this lone freighter to dock. Note the railroad cars in the foreground on the quayside waterfront. *Britton Collection*

Left: the long gone Fulton Fishing Fleet in March 1964. Behind is the Brooklyn Bridge. *Britton Collection*

Below: A scene from yesteryear of a gas lamp on the Brooklyn Bridge in 1958. *Earl Osborn/Britton Collection.*

Left: A small oil tanker makes a cautious approach toward the Brooklyn Bridge under the Manhattan Bridge on Christmas Eve 1958. *Earl Osborn/Britton Collection*

America's favourite boat ride, Circle Line. The *Circle Line IV* is packed with day trippers having had a tour of the harbour, including watching the sailing of the SS *France* in August 1969. *Britton Collection*

A close-up view of the Hudson River Day Line *Alexander Hamilton* focusing on those funnels and the lifeboat deck on 4 August 1963. Young children intending to travel would be bubbling over with excitement at this point as they waited to board the Hudson side-wheeler. *Britton Collection*

Flags gently fluttering in the summer breeze on board the *Alexander Hamilton*. *Britton Collection*

A delightful view taken from Dunderburg Mountain of the Hudson River Day Line *Alexander Hamilton* plying her way along the Hudson River past Anthony's Nose Mountain on 1 August 1970. *Britton Collection*

Looking from Storm King Mountain, we can see the *Alexander Hamilton* packed with day trippers from New York on the Hudson River in late February 1967. *Britton Collection*

Above left: The Hudson River Day Line *Alexander Hamilton* pauses briefly at Pughkeepsie as New York day trippers alight for a picnic on the banks of the Hudson river. *Britton Collection*

Above right: The *City of Keansburg* casts a golden reflection in the East River on the 12 September 1959. *Britton Collection*

Left: Passengers line up to board the Hudson steamers *City of Keansburg* and *John A. Meseck* at Battery Landing, New York on 4 August 1955. *Britton Collection*

The post-war transatlantic boom saw the introduction of the 642ft-long *Statendam* in 1957, which was equipped with accommodation for 84 first-class and 868 tourist-class passengers. The third liner of the Holland America Line fleet was the *Rotterdam*, which could accommodate 301 first and 1,055 tourist-class passengers. When she first entered New York Harbor, onlookers were amazed at her unusual design which lacked a traditional funnel, instead having twin uptakes for the exhausts.

Following the departure of the Holland America Line, the piers became the base for a Portuguese freighter firm, but sadly they were subsequently destroyed by a fire. The charred and rusting remains were later demolished.

Todd Shipyard and Bethlehem Steel Yard

All ships and ocean liners require regular maintenance to keep them seaworthy and New York provided some outstanding repair facilities. After the Second World War there were six large shipyards, but by the 1980s this had reduced to just two. The Todd Shipyard in Weehawken, New Jersey were just across from the mid-Manhattan shore. The shipyard had a magnetic attraction to enthusiasts, curious to discover what hidden gems were under repair.

Perhaps one of the most interesting repair facilities were the floating dry docks. The New York floating docks were like a pontoon, possessing floodable buoyancy chambers and a 'U'-shape cross-section to cradle the vessel which was to be repaired. At the Todd Shipyard it was possible to observe a ship being gradually moved into position by local tugboats. The valves on the floating dry dock would be opened, allowing the tanks to fill with water and causing the dry dock to float lower in the water. After the deck submerged the ship would manoeuvre into position inside the floating dry dock cradle. After securing the ship under repair, the water in the floating dry dock tanks would be pumped out and the dry dock would gradually rise, allowing the ship to be lifted clear of the water. Wedges would then be knocked into position on the hull of the ship making it stable enough for work to commence.

On occasions even large liners have suddenly appeared at Todd's for emergency repairs, notably the Italian Line *Michelangello*, which had sustained severe storm damage in 1966 after being ripped apart by 60ft waves; Cunard's *Britannic*, which suffered a fractured crank shaft; and *Ocean Monarch*, which entered dry dock with a twisted propeller.

The largest dry dock in New York was at the 56th Street yards of Bethlehem Steel in Brooklyn. The American Export Line passenger giants *Constitution* and *Independence* would use this facility during the off-peak season for their annual refits. This would include examination of the hull, prop shafts and propellers, de-scaling and a full repaint. If one was lucky enough to obtain entry into the dry dock on such occasions it was possible to marvel at the sheer size of an ocean liner. To peer up from ground level was just astounding and never to be forgotten. When the 56th Street facilities closed in the mid-1960s the operations transferred to Bethlehem Steel Hoboken yard.

Kearny Scrapyards

A destination in New York for all shipping enthusiasts was, and continues to be, the Kearny scrapyards, some 15 miles west of Manhattan, along the west banks of the Hackensack River. Visitors are not always welcome and may be greeted by howling guard dogs. Although a depressing location to visit, the graveyards of New York shipping are a must to visit. The sound of the wrecker's clanking cranes rings in the ears and the smell of metal being torched fills the nostrils, leaving a scar on the memory. Here was the last resting place of many fine vessels: ocean liners, naval vessels, rusting tugs, redundant New York ferries and floating cranes.

For many there was and is an attraction to the Kearney scrapyards to purchase and save a memento from a favourite ship or tug. In fact, many retired naval officers have been observed removing items from the bridge of a favourite ship they served on as she is stripped for demolition. At the time of writing, the author has his eyes on the funnel of a redundant railroad tug boat, if his wife permits!

During the Second World War the Kearny scrapyards were a shipbuilding facility as a major shipbuilder for the Federal Shipyards. At the end of the war the military contracts suddenly dried up and so the shipbuilding changed to ship breaking. This operation expanded enormously in the 1970s, when the government decided to dispose of the reserve 'Dead Fleet'. Once again the fortunes of the yards changed in the 1990s, when risks from asbestos became more widely known and scrapping contracts were awarded to India, China and Pakistan. The yards reduced down to just one wrecking crane and pier with a vastly slimmed down workforce. At the time of writing there remain some decaying nautical hidden gems awaiting the cutter's torch, but the future prospects still remain uncertain.

BROOKLYN

Pier 1, Fulton Street, Orient Overseas Line

Beginning in the 1960s Orient Overseas Line operated services from Pier 1 at Fulton Street in Brooklyn on the long-haul New York-Panama/Far East service. The company was founded in 1947 by the late C.Y. Tung. Tung dreamed of creating the first international Chinese merchant fleet. From 1947 the Orient Overseas Line began operating with all-Chinese crews and the company purchased redundant NDL and Hamburg American Line vessels for cargo and passenger operations.

In 1969 the company changed its name to Orient Overseas Container Line (OOCL) and was the first Asian shipping line to transport containers. Meanwhile, C.Y. Tung had other ambitions and when he purchased the former RMS *Queen Elizabeth* he set about converting her into a floating university in Hong Kong Harbour. As the liner neared completion he renamed her *Seawise University*, with plans to sail her around the Pacific and possibly into New York. However, on 9 January 1972 the great liner caught fire and sank as a total loss. Subsequently OOCL have successfully specialised in containerisation operations.

Pier 4, US Army Terminal, Military Transportation Service

Pier 4 was known to generations of US service personnel as a point of departure and the place where they stepped ashore and were home. The 95-acre complex between 58th and 63rd Street in Brooklyn was made up of busy piers, docks, warehouses, cranes, railroad and cargo transfer facilities. During the Second World War these facilities were vital to the war effort in Europe and North Africa in the defeat of Adolf Hitler's Nazi forces. Approximately 85 per cent of army equipment and US forces departed from this terminal, many never to return.

The former US Army Military Terminal in Brooklyn is architecturally and historically important as it was designed by Cass Gilbert in 1918. It was therefore listed on the National Register of Historic Places in 1983 as an example of modern industrial design using reinforced concrete construction.

By the mid-1970s the Military Sea Transportation Service (MSTS) had declined and began to phase out troopships in favour of aircraft. Many of the fleet of US Army vessels using Pier 4 were subsequently mothballed. The site was closed and sold to the city of New York in 1981.

21st Street Pier, Bull Line

Bull Line, or more correctly Bull-Insular Line, was a bit of an oddity in New York as its fleet by and large consisted of freighters with a facility to carry between four and twelve passengers. This shipping line took its name from Archibald H. Bull, who was the founder of the British-flagged New York & Porto Rico Steamship Company in 1885. The Bull Line was established in 1902 to serve the US Atlantic coastwise trade to Puerto Rico.

After the Second World War, Bull Line identified an opportunity to develop a service between New York, San Juan and Ciudad Trujillo. It invested in the purchase of an 18-year-old ship which was renamed *Puerto Rico*. The refurbished ship had accommodation for 200 first-class passengers and sailed from the 21st Street Pier at New York on a fortnightly schedule. It soon became apparent that her running costs, lack of freight capacity and competition made her operation unsustainable and by 1951 she was laid up.

In 1956 Bull's heirs sold out to American Coal Shipping and in 1961 Bull Line was sold on to the Greek shipping magnet Manuel K. Kulukundis. Some say the Bull Line name was jinxed, for in 1963 all the Kulukundis companies went bankrupt. Overnight the familiar Bull Line flag, with its white swallow-tailed pennant bordered in red with a blue initial B, disappeared from the New York scene.

33rd Street Pier, Farrell Lines

The Farrell Lines, with its flag of a white cross with fields of alternate red and blue quarters set on a buff black-topped funnel, docked at the 1,000ft-long pier at 33rd Street Pier. Every Friday at least three Farrell Lines ships would sail from New York to far-off destinations in the south Atlantic.

Farrell Lines can trace its origins back to 1910, when James Farrell established his own steamship company, the Isthmian Steamship Company. Farrell was the son of a ship's captain and his knowledge and experience resulted in a great shipping industry success. By 1928 he had expanded with involvement in several shipping companies: Argonaut Lines, Robin Lines and American South African Lines. Both of James Farrell's sons went on to develop the shipping investments, but in 1940 John Farrell abolished Argonaut Lines and transferred its vessels to American South African

Lines (ASAL) to operate a service from New York to Africa. In 1948 ASAL changed its name to Farrell Lines.

In 1965 Farrell Lines ceased operating passenger services and switched its attention entirely to the movement of cargo.

The Farrell Lines office, high up on the fourteenth floor in downtown Manhattan, was always an exciting place to visit. As one entered the office behind the receptionist there was a huge map of the world with chains of white lights pinpointing the various trade routes served by the Farrell Lines. Visitors were guaranteed a warm welcome by the wheelchair-bound MD, John J. Farrell, who would make sure adults were refreshed with a cup of coffee and younger enthusiasts were given an ice-cold coca cola. John Farrell would then give an office tour, showing off his scale models of ships and his paintings. On departing, visitors' pockets were stuffed full of publicity leaflets and interesting goodies. Each Christmas John Farrell would distribute a two-week holiday bonus cheque to all his employees with a warm handshake and smile. This genuine warmth made Farrell Lines one of the most popular shipping employers in New York.

Above: Cold duty picket stands alone with his 'No Contract, No Work' billboard during the Longshoreman's Strike of January 1963. *Associated Press*

Right: The Whitehall Terminal in 1949. *Britton Collection*

The arrival of the
St George ferry
Miss New York
in 1948. *Britton
Collection*

With a Moran Towing Company tugboat as her escort, the French Line SS *Liberté* drifts into New York Harbor and looks a spectacular sight from the air. *World Ship Society*

EAST RIVER

Pier 15, Maiden Lane, Spanish Line

Visitors in the 1950s and early 1960s to Pier 15 to meet arrivals or watch sailings of the SS *Covadona* and SS *Guadalupa* from/to Spain will have distinct memories of flamboyant sailors shouting out loud instructions in fast-speaking Spanish. These fiery gentlemen worked for the Compania Transatlantica Espanola (CTE), known to New Yorkers simply as the Spanish Line. Local Spanish speakers popularly referred to the company as La Transatlantica.

La Transatlantica was established in 1850 as Compania de Vapores Corrreos A Lopez and began operations with a 400-ton sailing paddlewheel steamer. By 1894 the company had expanded the fleet to thirty-three vessels.

Following the First World War the Spanish Line embarked on considerable expansion and modernisation of the fleet with the construction of some luxurious ocean-going ships. This was disrupted by the Spanish Civil War and a large proportion of the fleet was destroyed or damaged beyond economic repair. For political reasons those vessels that were named after Spanish royalty were renamed. After the Second World War the Spanish Line partially recovered lost ground with regular services to Pier 15 in New York.

In 1960 it was proposed to transform the shipping line into an airline, but financial backing was not forthcoming. Between 1960 and 1974 the shipping fleet went into terminal decline and was engaged in minor shipping operations using leased vessels. Shortly before writing these words in 2013, the remains of the once-proud Spanish Line entered an insolvency procedure. One notable legacy of the Spanish Line for New Yorkers is the taste of Spanish wine, which was a welcome import from the holds of docking ships.

FULTON FISH MARKET FISHING FLEET

An often overlooked part of the local scene on the Hudson River and in New York Harbor was the Fulton fishing fleet. Amongst their number were the shad fishing boats, which were quite remarkable and had distinctive square-shaped sterns. After netting their catches, the fleet would descend on Fulton Fish Market to land them near the Brooklyn Bridge along the East River waterfront. This was also the destination of many fishing boats from across the Atlantic Ocean.

Jim Gavin's glorious portrait picture of the SS *Britanis*, with the Empire State Building behind, on 18 June 1982. The SS *Britanis* was built in 1931 and entered into service on 3 June 1932, sailing for Matson Lines as the SS *Montery*. She saw active war service as the USAT *Montery*. She was sold for scrap in July 2000. On her final voyage to the Indian scrap yard she broke free of the tugboat towing her and sank. *Jim Gavin/Britton Collection*

The Moran tugboat *Doris Moran* is rapidly approaching the port side bow to assist the American Export Line SS *Constitution* to turn in the Hudson River towards the Atlantic Ocean on 8 June 1954. *Britton Collection*

A low-flying helicopter buzzes the Cunard RMS *Franconia* as she manoeuvres in the Hudson River in June 1971. The *Franconia* entered service for Cunard in 1955, originally named as RMS *Ivernia* of the Saxonia Class ocean liners. In 1963 she was rebuilt as a cruise ship and renamed. The *Franconia* remained in service for Cunard until being withdrawn and laid up for sale at Southampton in 1971. *Britton Collection*

The fresh fish would be sold at the Fulton wholesale market to restaurateurs and retailers. It became the most important fish wholesale in the USA, with sold fish packed in ice and rushed off by rail for distribution across the country. Until relocation in 2005, the Fulton Fish Market was the oldest fish market in continuous operation in one place.

From the mid-1960s the local fishing fleet began to dwindle. Fish began to be flown in from all parts of the world and then trucked to the Fulton Fish Market. Boats from the Atlantic began to dock and land their catches in New Jersey and Long Island to ship via container trucks. Memories of dozens of Fulton fishing boats along the East River are now becoming distant.

Pier 81, New York Circle Line, the Hudson River Day Line

The Circle Line can trace its origins back to 1908, when a steamer named the *Tourist* owned by Captain John Roberts offered a sightseeing cruise around Manhattan. However, it was not until after the Second World War that a number of competing boat excursion companies merged to form the Circle Line Company. Circle Line quickly established itself and gained a fine reputation for providing one of the most famous tourist boat rides in the world around New York Harbor, offering magnificent views of the Manhattan skyline all year round. The company branded itself with the marketing slogan, 'America's Favourite Boat Ride'. Circle Line offered 35-mile cruises around the harbour, turning into the East River off the Battery, before cruising along the Upper Harlem River and passing Luxury Liner Row. From the decks of these Circle Line boats many superb colour slides, photographs and films have been shot of the liners at rest.

By 1950 the operation began to expand the fleet to include larger vessels, including the *Calypso*, a converted Second World War boat with a famous past. In 1955 Circle Line moved from Battery Park to Pier 83, West 42nd Street. By 1961 Circle Line recorded its 10 millionth passenger and the following year Circle Line acquired the Hudson River Day Line. Sailing from Pier 81, on West 41st Street, the magnificent Hudson River Day Line steamers sailed up the Hudson River to Bear Mountain State Park and West Point, before turning back at Poughkeepsie without docking. The service was maintained by a distinguished fleet of paddle-steamers or 'side-wheelers' as they were known locally and this lasted up until 1971, when the *Alexander Hamilton* was withdrawn from service because of the high operational costs of the fuel and the fifty-five-man crew. She was replaced by the efficient and economic diesel-powered *Dayliner*, with a crew of forty-three.

The *Alexander Hamilton*, with her twin funnels and flags fluttering from ten flag poles, had plied the Hudson River for forty-five seasons, carrying up to 4,000 passengers per voyage. She was a beautiful ship and was equipped with a 3,400 horsepower inclined reciprocating steam engine. Built in 1924 at the Bethlehem Steel Corporation of Sparrows Point, the *Alexander Hamilton* was the last of the Hudson River Day Line side-wheelers. She was therefore a perfect candidate for preservation. The *Alexander Hamilton* was set to commence her retirement with a new career as a restaurant at the newly opened South Street Seaport Museum in New York. It was quickly realised that the embryonic museum could not finance such a demanding project and the redundant Hudson River Day Line side-wheeler was moved across the East River to the Brooklyn Navy Yard, prior to being laid up at the Harbourside Terminal in Jersey City.

In 1974 the *Alexander Hamilton* was purchased by the Railroad Pier Company of Middletown Township for conversion into a restaurant, but was vandalised; a puncture in the hull caused the old lady to partially capsize and she settled on a mud bank. A group of former crew members and enthusiasts formed the Alexander Hamilton Preservation Society and

had the vessel placed on the National Register of Historic Sites. This entitled the vessel to financial assistance through Federal Funding. New owners, the Sulko Pier Enterprises, took possession of the *Alexander Hamilton* and on 15 September 1977 she was refloated. Great plans were in place to restore the ship to her former glory at Weehawken. The US Navy assisted

Above and below: If only pictures could record the wonderful 'clap, clap' sound of the paddle wheels as the Hudson River Day Line *Alexander Hamilton* is pictured approaching Poughkeepsie on 10 August 1963. *Britton Collection*

This picture of the Hudson River Day Line Pier 81 conjures up interest with a fine line-up of classic cars. This was the starting point for a glorious day trip on the *Alexander Hamilton* up the Hudson. *Braun Brothers/Britton Collection*

and allowed the *Alexander Hamilton* to tie up at the weapons pier at Earle, Leonardo in New Jersey, ready for a US Coast Guard inspection prior to being towed through New York Harbor.

During a storm on the night of 7 November 1977, the *Alexander Hamilton* sank in 16ft of water whilst tied up at the Navy Pier. The wreck of this famous vessel was left to rot until she became just a steel skeleton – a disgrace to a nation which craves heritage and history!

Other frequent callers at Pier A, Battery Park and later Pier 81 were the magnificent 1926-built excursion boats *City of Keansburg* and her sister the *City of New York*. The 231ft twin-funnel *City of Keansburg* was built for the Delaware & New York Steamboat Company (popularly known as the Keansburg Steamboat Company) at the Newburgh shipyard of Harry A. Marvel & Co. She was propelled by two sets of

750hp three-cylinder triple-expansion engines powered by two oil-fired 250psi water tube steam boilers. At one time the magnificent *City of Keansburg* carried 2,036 passengers on three round-trips a day to New Point Comfort Beach in Keansburg, New Jersey. These services ceased when the Keansburg Steamboat Pier was destroyed by Hurricane Donna on 12 September 1960. The *City of Keansburg* transferred operations to an Atlantic Highland pier until it was destroyed by fire on 6 May 1965. Thereafter she saw out her remaining years on harbour excursions until laid up in 1968.

A failed attempt was made to convert the *City of Keansburg* into a floating restaurant in Florida. One of her triple-expansion steam engines was removed for display at Allaire State Park, but her remains are forgotten and abandoned, rotting away derelict in the St John's River.

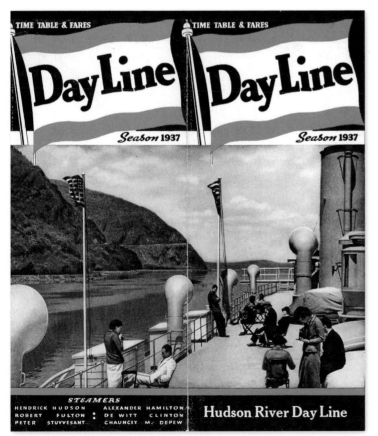

A Hudson Day Line brochure.

The US Reserve Fleet – 'The Dead Fleet'

Locals would whisper to visiting shipping enthusiasts to New York, 'Have you seen the Dead Fleet?' Whatever were they referring to? The answer to this question laid anchored some 40 miles north-west of New York on the west bank of the Hudson River.

After the Second World War in 1946 Congress established the Hudson River National Defence Fleet near Haverstraw, which comprised a sizeable fleet of surplus ships. In 1965 there were 189 vessels anchored and chained together systematically in rows of ten, anchored bow and stern. The lines of ships extended from Jones Point dock to the south near Tomkins Cove. This curiosity attracted hundreds of unofficial visitors who would drive up Route 9W on a Sunday afternoon and secretly snap a picture.

Amongst the Dead Fleet were several former commercial ships, complete with their funnel markings. These vessels were under charter to the likes of the American Export Lines and Moore-McCormack. Looking through binoculars, it was possible to identify many old veteran Liberty ships and one or two hidden treasures like the pre-war liners *Manhattan* and *Washington*.

At times ships would disappear down the Hudson for a refit and further service. During the Korean War 130 vessels were pressed back into service with just thirty-nine ships remaining at anchor. At the conclusion of hostilities many were to return to the Reserve Fleet only to be recalled in 1956 during the Suez Crisis. Again the Dead Fleet entered a period of hibernation until the Vietnam War, when more than forty ships were reactivated.

The fleet was not exclusively used for military purposes and when the US Department of Agriculture required extra storage space for reserves of government-owned wheat, the Hudson River Reserve Fleet was called upon as a temporary secure refuge. In the following decade more than 53 million bushels of wheat were stored on 231 ships. This became a regular practice between 1953 and 1963. It was amusing for observers to spot when ships had been unloaded of wheat as they rose 20ft higher, exposing a bright band of orange rust. In order to preserve wheat for longer periods of storage, a ventilation system was installed in the ships. This facility, it is said, saved the US Government almost $5 million on secure commercial storage costs.

The Dead Fleet was maintained by a watch of eighty-six men and was valued at over $255 million. The regular maintenance programme involved coating surfaces with preservative and greasing up exposed parts.

Periodically machinery was turned over and observers would witness a cloud of black smoke billowing from the funnels when this happened. Generators and electrical equipment were cleaned and coated with an anti-fungus varnish. The exteriors of ships were sprayed with a grey preservative annually and the hulls protected from corrosion by an 'electric current cathodic protection' device, pioneered by the Royal Navy.

The costs of maintaining the Hudson Reserve Fleet and providing security patrols was escalating by the late 1960s and a decision was made to reduce and eventually dispose of the fleet. Ships began to be sold for scrap and those to be retained were transferred to James River. The last two ships to be towed away for scrapping in Spain, the *Edwin M. Stanton* and the *Earl A. Bloomquist*, departed on 8 July 1971 and the site was closed.

Pictured near Indian Park in August 1956, we see the Hudson River Day Line *Alexander Hamilton* packed with day trippers from New York passing the 'Dead Fleet'. *Britton Collection*

TRIBUTE TO THE TUGBOATS

The tugboats of New York Harbor have always had an international reputation for raw, rugged power. Their crews are known as masters of all work, whether it be docking an enormous Atlantic passenger liner or the movement of railroad barges. They had a reputation of being able to work well as teams with a warm and friendly approach, often with a great sense of humour.

New York tugboats were of distinctive style with tall, narrow bridge houses. This design was to aid in visual navigation whenn looking over the tops of the railroad boxcars on the barges towed alongside 'on the hip'. The strong currents of the Hudson River demanded that their unseen marine steam engines and later diesel engines were strong and reliable.

Whilst the Moran fleet was the largest in New York, closely followed by McAllisters, they were by no means the only tugboat operators. Tugs of the Meseck, Dalzell, Esso, the US Navy, Coast Guard, Army Engineers and railroad companies could be seen scurrying around the port.

After the American Civil War New York became a major termini for many railroads, including the Erie, Pennsylvania, B&O and Lackawanna. The geographical problem that presented itself in the transfer of passengers and freight to Manhattan was the Hudson River. Ferries took passengers over to the

New Jersey side to board westbound trains. Freight transfer was more complex and the solution was to load railroad box cars on to car floats or railroad barges which could be towed by tugboats. Each railroad built freight transfer sheds with dolly ramps to propel/unload the railroad box cars. To move the barges around the port the railroads commissioned their own tug fleets.

In the mid-1930s, during the golden age of transatlantic passenger liners, there were over 700 steam tugs operating in New York, with over 600,000 railroad box cars being moved around the harbour annually. Additionally the Brooklyn Navy Yard had its own fleet of tugs to handle naval vessels. The City of New York also had a small fleet of tugs for hauling 'garbage scow barges' containing the city's refuge and waste which was towed out to sea and dumped into the Atlantic Ocean beyond the Narrows.

Perhaps the most famous railroad tugboats operating in New York were those of the New York Central Railroad. The New York Central served most of the north-east, including the extensive network of lines in New York which connected with Boston, Chicago and the Midwest. The New York Central's Grand Central Terminal is one of the best-known landmarks in New York. The railroad's tugs were distinctive as they had a black funnel with a red wrap-around badge proudly proclaiming the words, 'New York Central'. The superstructure of the tugs above the hull was a mustard green livery, which stood out when they were about their regular duties of car float operation.

The names of Moran and McAllister became synonymous with the tugboat industry of New York Harbor. The Moran Towing & Transportation Company was founded by Michael Moran in 1860 and is by far the oldest and largest tugboat company in the United States. The Moran tugs are instantly recognisable by the white 'M' painted on their black funnels. They pioneered the development of the tugboat from steam to diesel and through their experience working in New York Harbor have solved every type of towing problem. Their fine reputation spread and over the years they expanded and developed to handle large-scale ocean-towing operations.

During the Second World War, Moran Towing operated more than 100 tugs, both Moran- and government-owned. Moran made a significant contribution to the war effort by towing huge barges across the Atlantic. Moran tugs also towed the artificial Mulberry Harbours across the English Channel to strategic points in Normandy, France to facilitate the rapid offloading of military supplies during the Allied Invasion.

The first McAllisters enterprise was started during the American Civil War by James McAllister in 1864. The McAllister partnership was formed in 1898 and it purchased a shipyard in Newtown Creek, just south of Greenpoint Avenue Bridge. The construction of a fleet of tugboats commenced to specialise in salvage operations. During the two world wars McAllister transported large cargoes of tanks and ammunition and became specialists in handling high explosives. McAllister expanded and acquired the Card Towing Company and the Lee Transit Company (both of New York) in 1944, the P.F. Martin Company of Philadelphia in 1949 and Ainsley Towing in 1951, adding to their tug and barge fleet. The shrewd McAllisters Board also acquired Russell Brothers with their fleet of tugs and barges in 1961, which placed them in the forefront of the oil transportation business.

New York tugboats have increased in power over the years, but their 100ft length remains the same. After the Second World War the steam tug fleet began to rapidly demise, being replaced by boats with diesel propulsion. Tug duties would typically begin at daybreak with a docking or undocking operation between the Narrows and 72nd Street, North River. In foggy weather, tugs would venture down into the Lower Bay in New York Harbor to guide shipping through the Ambrose Channel. The work of towing the great Atlantic liners in and out of port was usually reserved for Moran Towing tugs.

With the introduction of 2,000hp diesel tugs, the operation of docking and undocking the Cunard Queen liners required only six Moran tugs. For the SS *United States* and French Line SS *Liberté*, only five tugs were normally allocated to the job, while the Holland America Line SS *Nieuw Amsterdam* required only four tugs. The tug numbers were strengthened, however, if high winds or strong currents so determined. Each team of tugs works under the direction of a docking pilot, usually from the Reynolds Pilots Association who specialise in docking large ocean liners in New York. Once docking/undocking is complete, the liners were piloted by Sandy Hook Association Pilots who guided them out through the Ambrose Channel and beyond the Narrows. On occasions, when the weather conditions were very rough, it was not unknown for Sandy Hook pilots to be unable to transfer from the liner down a Jacob's ladder to a pilot boat. When this happened the pilot would have no other choice than to remain aboard for a voyage to Europe!

On average it took up to twenty-five years for a New York tugboat captain to qualify as a docking pilot. He would have to gain considerable experience, knowledge and, above all, confidence in the docking process.

Additionally he would have to be fully aware of the varying tides and currents of the Hudson, which at times could be frozen over or have an ice flow. When docking a Cunard Queen liner at Piers 90 or 92 the docking pilot had to have a complete understanding of what leverage to apply from the team of assisting tugs. The routine was to usually have four tugs fasten with their lines to the bow and two tugs linked by rope hawsers to the stern. At given commands by whistle (later radio) the tugs would push or pull.

The qualification period for a Sandy Hook pilot was usually fifteen years. The Sandy Hook pilot had to be proficient in the lights, buoys, fog signals, charts, soundings, rules of the road, fixing positions, radar, gyro, tides, customs regulations, immigration regulations, Morse code, semaphore, rope, wire and canvas work, maritime law, weather conditions and shipping propulsion. Above all, the Sandy Hook pilot when working with the great Atlantic ocean liners and cruise ships had to be very brave in climbing the Jacob's ladder at the point of transfer and act calmly but with authority in a 'gentlemanly way' on the bridge of these liners. When qualified, the Sandy Hook pilot had to be accompanied by an experienced pilot in and out to sea for the first six months. Written and oral testing was then given before the newly qualified Sandy Hook pilot was given a 20ft license, which limited his pilot work to vessels drawing 20ft or less. For the next seven years this draft licence was increased annually until he was fully qualified to pilot an Atlantic liner. This very demanding and skilled training made Sandy Hook pilots perhaps the best qualified in the world.

There were occasions, however, when the services of the pilots and tugboats in New York were unused by the commodores and captains of the Atlantic liners. On one such occasion Cunard's Captain David Sorrell shot to fame as relieving captain on the *Queen Mary* in 1953 when he famously docked the *Queen Mary* without the aid of tugs or a docking pilot in New York. Captain Sorrell said that the night prior to entering New York he had received a message asking if it was possible to take the *Queen Mary* into New York and dock her at Pier 90 without the aid of tugs or a docking pilot. 'Certainly, I will be delighted,' he replied. For five days the whole of the Port of New York had been paralysed by the strike of 3,500 tug men who were seeking a pay rise. Captain Sorrell revealed that for years he had planned three methods as to how he would dock the *Queen Mary* unaided. With the quayside packed with over 2,000 spectators watching and anticipating disaster, the *Queen Mary* headed cautiously up the fast-flowing River Hudson with its challenging tides. Additionally there was also the risk of strong gusts of wind which could have a tremendous effect on the sheer size of the liner. Amongst the crowd were many of the striking tug men who could quickly identify any signs of trouble. As the *Queen Mary* approached Pier 90 even the traffic on the highway stopped. Everyone waited nervously, many with cameras at the ready.

In an interview with the author, Captain Sorrell remembered that the morning was hot and muggy, but the crucial factor was that there was little, if any, wind. To assist him in calculating the precise course of the liner, he had to hand his homemade wooden setsquare with a semi-circle of screws on top. A lifeboat from the Cunard *Caronia* was sent out to assist with docking lines and, with the tide right, Captain Sorrell began to manoeuvre the *Queen Mary* towards the entrance to Pier 90. At 09.50 the *Queen Mary* began to slowly pass the end of the pier. A minute later the lifeboat from the *Caronia* caught a mooring line and this was quickly secured to the end of Pier 90. All appeared to be going well, but Captain Sorrell recalled that he suddenly felt the underwater currents of the River Hudson grip the stern of the liner and swing her dangerously towards the pier. To counter this, Sorrell ordered, 'Back all go astern' and with one whistle she responded immediately. 'I backed out in a hurry,' the smiling Captain Sorrell recollected.

Plan 2 now went into action. Captain Sorrell waited for slack water between the tides and to do this he observed the movement of driftwood and debris in the River Hudson. Checking with his setsquare, he noted down readings and decided it was time to lower the port anchor. He revealed that his plan was to use the tide to his advantage. He was going to use the corner of the pier as a pivot, lay the liner prow on it, and bend the *Queen Mary* round, using the current to ease the stern around. He commenced this operation at 10.10 a.m. and within five minutes the bow had been secured to allow the *Queen Mary*'s capstans to pull them taut. At this point Captain Sorrell felt a great relief for within five minutes the great liner was making progress into the slip. A further five minutes passed and a line astern had been secured and further lines were attached to make her secure. The 976 passengers who were lining the rails to watch the hazardous docking suddenly burst into spontaneous applause and began cheering. The quartermaster Ken Furr and officers congratulated him and shook his hand. Going out onto the flying bridge Captain Sorrell noticed that a strong southerly wind had sprung up; had it occurred just minutes earlier it would have potentially caused a great disaster.

Captain David Sorrell modestly related that no one could have guessed how much worldwide publicity this would generate and the following twenty-four hours after the docking were the most hectic of his life with

requests for radio, television and newspaper interviews. Captain Sorrell also sailed unassisted from New York.

The modern cruise liners that call into New York today now rarely require the assistance of tugs as they are fitted with bow and stern thrusters, which can manoeuvre them safely into the dock.

For some years there has been an annual New York Harbor tugboat race. This may have its origins in the International Maritime Week and creation of the Waterfront Commission of New York Harbor in 1953, when many of the New York tugboats competed in a 2-mile race. Nowadays the contest for working tugs is held every autumn, on the Sunday before Labour Day. Tugs race for one nautical mile from 79th Street to Pier 84 at 44th Street. Other events include: nose-to-nose pushing competitions, a line toss competition and a costume contest between the crews.

The *City of Keansburg* languishes at Martha's Vineyard, McAllister Brothers Yard, facing an uncertain future, on 18 May 1985. *Britton Collection*

The 1961-built, single-screw, 2,000-horsepower McAllister tug *Brian A. McAllister* joins her teammate tug *McAllisters Bros* to assist dock an American Export freighter into Hoboken. *Britton Collection*

Alexandra McAllister is heading somewhere in a great hurry along the Hudson River and pushing up quite a bow wave on 9 September 1980. *Jim Gavin*

Rays of sunlight fall on the United States Line SS *America* as she is escorted up the Hudson by Moran Towing tugboats to Pier 86. *Britton Collection*

The steam tugboats *Capt. C. Mathiasen*, built in 1919, *Helen M. Mathiasen* and *Willard S. Carroll* are pictured trapped in the ice-bound Mathiasen Tug Terminal in October 1947. *Britton Collection*

The steam tug *Edith Mathiasen*, built in 1892, awaits her next turn of duty at the foot of Baltic Street in 1948. *Britton Collection*

Steam tugs galore! Here is a sight for steam tug enthusiasts everywhere – the Mathiasen Tug Terminal, Baltic Street, in July 1948. *Britton Collection*

New York Fireboats

Purpose-built fireboats in New York have been a feature of the harbour since as long ago as 1809. Volunteer fire fighters in New York are said to have mounted a rotary engine on a whaleboat and it became known as 'Coffee Mill'. The concept of a floating and mobile fire appliance was a direct response to the problem that a land-based fire appliance would be unable to tackle a fire on a vessel docked at any of New York's finger piers. In 1874 the Fire Commissioners of New York awarded a contract for the construction of the first full time and fully equipped fireboat, the wooden-hulled, steam-powered *William F Havemeyer*.

During the early part of the twentieth century New York Harbor suffered two significant disasters. The first was a fire at the NDL pier at Hoboken in New Jersey on 30 June 1900, resulting in the loss of over 400 lives. Four years later, on 15 June 1904, the PS *General Slocum* caught fire and sank in the East River. At the time of the fire she was on a charter to carry members of St Mark's Evangelical Lutheran Church to a church picnic. An estimated 1,021 people of the 1,342 perished. The disaster motivated Federal and State regulation to improve the emergency equipment on US passenger ships and liners. It also led to considerable improvements with the provision of fireboats in New York Harbor. From this point a fleet of fireboats was created and today the city can boast perhaps the best-equipped fast-response fireboats in the world, capable of pumping 50,000 gallons of water per minute, with advanced technology to fight potential chemical terrorist attacks on New York shipping.

One of the most impressive traditional displays by the New York fireboats occurs when a new vessel enters port on a maiden voyage or when a liner or ship departs for the final time. The fireboats anchor off the Battery in salute and spray out huge plumes of water. Repeat performances are given annually at the harbour festivals and at such occasions red, white and blue dye is added to the spray.

In the mid-1960s it was possible to contact the Marine Administration Unit at Pier 1, North River and arrange to view the following fireboats on station at the locations listed:

H. Sylvia A.H.G. Wilks	Foot of Fulton Street, East River, Brooklyn
John D. McKean	Pier A, North River, New York
Senator Robert F. Wagner	Foot of 90th Street, East River, New York
Harry M. Archer MD	Foot of Grand Street, East River, New York
John J. Harvey	Pier 53, North River, Foot of Bloomfield Street, New York
Governor Alfred E. Smith	Foot of 52nd Street, Brooklyn, New York
Fire Fighter	Pier 6 Tompkinsville, Staten Island, New York
Smoke II (fire tender)	Pier A, North River, New York
John H. Glenn Jr	Army Pier, Little Harbor, Fort Totten, Bayside, Queens

In the 1960s the brave firefighting staff was always very welcoming to visitors and on rare occasions they have even taken shipping enthusiasts out on a fireboat for an unofficial test around New York Harbor!

Photographer Jim Gavin was in position bright and early to record this superb picture of a fireboat salute to the SS *Atlantic* which was heading out on her maiden voyage on 7 September 1983. *Britton Collection*

RAILROAD FERRIES

Ferries crossing the Hudson in New York have always been part of the local scene and to many they have been just part of the working day, at the beginning or end. Ferry services across the Hudson can be traced back to the eighteenth century, when services were powered by sail and oar between New York and New Jersey. During the nineteenth century they became more reliable with the introduction of paddlewheel steamboats. Routes and terminals were developed by the railroad companies: the New York Central's West Shore Line, the Central of New Jersey, Erie, Delaware, Pennsylvania, and the Lackawanna & Western. Impressive new buildings were built facing Manhattan on the Jersey side of the Hudson River. They quickly became very busy locations, packed with commuters during the morning and evening rush hours.

Hudson ferries contributed a critical role in the War of Independence and helped shape the local communities along the river. The ferries developed the marine use of the steam engine in the United States. Millions of immigrants can trace the first leg of their journey west on the ferries of the Hudson and it is fair to say that they have become established in American folklore.

The ferry routes across the Hudson expanded and developed until the mid-1920s, when approximately 27 million passengers were carried between New Jersey and Manhattan. After the opening of the Holland road tunnel on 12 November 1927 traffic on the Lackawanna ferries between Hoboken and 23rd Street declined by almost 40 per cent. The drop in ferry traffic continued after the opening of the George Washington Bridge on 25 October 1931 and the Lincoln Tunnel on 22 December 1937. This trend was to have an overall effect on ferry services and it was decided to close the Lackawanna's 23rd Street route on 31 December 1946 and the Christopher Street route on 30 March 1955. The Weehawken to West 42nd Street ferry was suspended in 1959.

A panoramic view taken from No. 90 Church Street in September 1952 looking across the Hudson over the Manhattan suburbia as the French Line SS *Ile de France* slowly makes her way up the North River. Note the Hudson steam ferries and the railroad car float ready to sail. *Britton Collection*

Between 1956 and 1960 the Erie Railroad merged its ferry and train operations with the Lackawanna at Hoboken Terminal. Non-economical weekend services on the Barclay Street route were suspended in February 1964 in an attempt to make ferry operations pay and make a profit. The Aldene Plan switched train services from the Central Railroad of New Jersey's waterfront terminal to terminate at Newark Penn Station or Pennsylvania Station, Manhattan. This resulted in the Liberty Street ferry closing on 25 April 1967.

When the Delaware & Hudson Railroad was absorbed into the Norfolk & Western system in 1967 it became apparent that the new management wanted rid of the deficit-ridden Erie–Lackawanna ferry operation. This service was being operated by just two old boats: *Elmira* and *Lackawanna*,

Left: Perhaps often overlooked subjects to photograph in New York were the support vessels. Here we see the Chapman's Century floating crane on 21 May 1966, awaiting her next turn of duty. *Britton Collection*

Below: There is something just so wonderful and exciting about the Hudson ferries and the Manhattan skyline that words cannot describe, but this stunning picture, taken in August 1964, says it all. *Britton Collection*

the survivors of a once mighty fleet of ferries numbering over 100 that once plied the North River for five railroad companies. The *Lackawanna* dated back to 1891 and had become particularly expensive to maintain as her hull plates had worn dangerously thin. The financial practicalities dictated that the railroad companies did not have the capital to replace the two ancient ferries and a decision was made to close the service, despite a daily passenger loading of over 3,000 passengers. The sad end came on 22 November 1967 at 5.45 p.m., when the *Lackawanna* headed from Barclay Street, New York to Hoboken for the final time followed, fifteen minutes later, by *Elmira*, the last steam ferry on the Hudson.

More than 100 ferry routes have come and gone on the Hudson River during the past century. Remarkably demographic trends linked to rail and road congestion have forced a change of thinking. Routes between New Jersey and Manhattan and Port Imperial, Weehawken and West 38th Street, with services between Peekshill, Garrison and West Point, are being restored. Today the Hudson is once again being criss-crossed by many ferry routes. The nostalgic high-pitched steam whistles of the Jersey Central and Pennsylvania Railroad and the romantic deep whistles of the Erie, Lackawanna and New York Central are now but distant memories, but the modern diesel ferries are highly efficient and more economical to operate.

The Lackawanna Railroad 23rd Street Ferry Pier in 1948. *Britton Collection*